Way to Love

A Commentary on the *Narad Bhakti Sutra*

Vaisnavacharya Chandan Goswami

Readers interested in the content matter of this book are invited to submit their queries to the following address:

Vaisnavacharya Chandan Goswami
Shanti Kutir
Radharaman Temple
Vrindavan
281121
U.P. India

innersmile108@gmail.com
www.shriradharaman.com

Second Edition

ISBN: 978-0-9891433-0-1
Library of Congress Control Number: 2013935746

To the Source of all inspiration, from time immemorial . . .

Preface

It's as though I have loved You infinite times, in infinite forms, life after life, forever. On the boat of my dreams, I have sailed down infinite rivers, entranced by their shimmering waves, compelled by their currents towards my ultimate destiny. And now I know the ocean of love gave its water as a gracious gift for each of those rivers. To the ocean all return.

There are unspoken prayers that echo in the heart like a single sustained note, supporting the melody of life. Today, some soul is praying, "I would ask nothing of You, but if You wish to bless me, grant me this. Make me a dolphin swimming freely in the ocean of Your heart. On the waves of Your joy, make me dance in Your love forever. Open my love-eyes so that I might see Your face in every face. I wish to hear Your Name in every sound and feel Your love in every heart, that I might be near You, my Love, everywhere and always."

It may seem unreasonable for a finite soul to try to bind the infinite Lord of all creation in her heart, like a child reaching out to catch the moon. But I have heard from the mouths of sages that Love makes the impossible possible. Love experiences what reason cannot know, and the heart can see visions that the eyes cannot see. With this hope we present Sage Narad's book of love to you. May this book open our eyes of love, forever.

Acknowledgements

The first day, when I started writing my commentary on the *Narad Bhakti Sutra*, I felt I was inadequate to write something about love. I turned to Lord Girdhari and prayed to Him to bestow this sacred work upon me and use me as His instrument to write the book. So, I am not the author but a mere channel, and the rightful Author is Lord Krishn. As His eternal servant, I am offering this book at His lotus feet, which are the everlasting shelter of my soul. What criticism shall I expect now, since this book is written by Him and offered to Him? I am blessed and always yearn that one day soon, my dear Lord will cast His lotus eyes upon me once again and call me to serve Him. But yes, I would like to acknowledge a few aspirants who are at His service and who have helped me to become adequate enough to attempt this work.

First of all, I pay my infinite obeisances to Sri Chaitanya Mahaprabhu, who allowed me to drown in the ocean of nectar. I pay my obeisances to my worshipful grandfather Sri Srimad Vishambhar Goswami, the guardian of the *Gaudiya Sampradaya*. With his blessings I am able to tread this path, and by his causeless mercy I can attempt to fulfil his innermost desire of spreading the Holy Name.

I pay my deepest respects to my parents Sri Srimad Padmanabh Goswami Maharaj and *Guru Mata* Saroj Goswami (my *Diksha* and *Shiksha Gurus*), who planted the seed of devotion in me and nourished me, so that I could blossom as a devotee.

I would like to thank Raakhee Modha, who encouraged me to write and complete this work so that people could understand the path of devotion in a simple way, though she would say her motives were selfish and she was craving for this blissful service. I know that it took many of her sleepless nights to complete the editing so that this book could be published. My love and gratitude will always extend to her.

I would like to thank Vishakha Dasi, who has helped us with the translations of verses and Vrajwasi poetries. I pray that one day she will reach that state of ecstasy where she will be able to serve Radha and Krishn in Their eternal abode. Finally, I am forever indebted to all of the ODev (Ocean of Devotion) devotees who have helped us throughout this project.

I know my offer of gratitude is insignificant in front of the efforts of these dear devotees and infinitesimal before the Love of the Lord, yet this beggar of love can only give the blessings inspired by his Beloved, as a gesture of profound appreciation. I revel in the joy these precious souls have given me through their tireless service.

Vaisnavacharya Chandan Goswami
Govardhan, Uttar Pradesh
Vijay Dasmi, 24 October 2012

Contents

1.	Introduction to Devotion	1
2.	Means to Attain Devotion	21
3.	The Essence of Devotion	41
4.	The Excellence of Devotion	59
5.	The Grace of Elevated Souls	86
6.	Overcoming Delusion	100
7.	Sacred Love	112
8.	Precautions	133
9.	Qualities of the Sacred Lover	148
10.	Union with the Beloved	172
Glossary		185
A List of the 84 Aphorisms in Sanskrit		189
A List of the 84 Aphorisms in English		193
Pronunciation Guide		199

1

Introduction to Devotion

Sutra 1

|| *hariḥ oṁ* || *athāto bhaktiṁ vyākhyāsyāmaḥ* ||

Therefore, we shall now explain devotion.

Sage Narad is an incarnation of Lord Krishn[1] who appeared in this world as a devotee to nourish mankind with devotion (*bhakti*). He revealed the following aphorisms[2] on devotion as the fruit of his own personal experience of union with the Beloved (the Lord).

Sage Narad gave a vow to Bhakti Devi (the goddess of devotion): "I will establish devotion in this world and prove its superiority over other paths (the path of action, the path of knowledge and the path of disciplined contemplation). If not, I will not be known as a devotee of Lord Krishn." (*Padma Puran*, *Srimad Bhagwatam Mahatmya* 2.14)

In this quote, the path of action is known as *karm yog*, where work is performed as a spiritual discipline. The path of knowledge (*gyan yog*) is most suited to intellectuals who want to study the *Veds*[3] in order to know their own true nature. The path of disciplined contemplation (*raj yog*) is a practice to still the wandering mind. The purpose of these aphorisms is to help aspirants understand the path of devotion (*bhakti yog*) through sacred love (*prem*),[4] which is exclusive and pure love for Lord Krishn. Narad assures the aspirant that this is a guaranteed path to attain Him.

There are four points to note from the first aphorism:

1. *Vishay* (the subject)

---

[1] Krishn is the Supreme Being, a complete incarnation, portrayed in the scriptures as a young Cowherd Boy.

[2] An aphorism is a saying, and the Sanskrit word for it is *Sutra*.

[3] *Veds* are the oldest scriptures in Hinduism.

[4] Sage Narad has his own definition of sacred love (*prem*), which will be explained from Chapter 7 onwards.

2. *Adhikari* (whom this doctrine is meant for)
3. *Prayojan* (the purpose)
4. *Sambandh* (the relationship)

1. The subject matter (*vishay*) of this doctrine is devotion.

2. Devotion is meant for those who have a yearning to understand and practice the path. Sage Narad says that his scripture is for anyone who has a belief in the existence of the Lord. To reach the first stage of devotion, the candidate must have faith. Faith means a solemn aspiration to attentively follow the process of devotion, as described in the scriptures.

The *Chaitanya Charitamrit* (2.22.64) states, "Only a person who has faith is eligible for devotion." Devotion does not depend on time, place, gender or caste. It is entirely dependent on faith. No one can fulfil any endeavour in any path without faith. In the *Bhagwad Gita* (17.28), Lord Krishn says, "Oblations, charity, austerities and other good works are futile if not done with faith because the performer will not receive the true fruit of his acts in this world or the next."

One can say faith means the removal of doubt combined with a favourable attitude towards the practice of devotion. The deeper a devotee's faith, the more his heart becomes favourably inclined. The devotee attempts to gain realisation from the scriptures and aspires to understand them logically. When there is firm faith in these teachings, one understands that life is wasted without the Lord, who is the soul's true goal.

Each scripture builds a firm foundation for a particular spiritual path and requires an aspirant to have specific qualifications, but in the scriptures of devotion, the path of devotion is open to all. Still, only those who want to shape their lives according to the *Narad Bhakti Sutra* are eligible to know it. People who are proud of their spiritual practice[5] and feel they do not need any guidance will not yearn to take shelter of this scripture. Those who are not satisfied with their understanding and practice of devotion, or those who are seeking the path which can make the Lord their Beloved, are eligible to follow the teachings of this scripture.

A person who wants to understand this path need not necessarily be a scholar. The purpose of devotion is not to satisfy one's intellectual

---

[5] Spiritual practice is devotional practice in the context of this doctrine.

curiosity. It is a subject that concerns one's life. Sage Narad is not addressing those who want to conduct an academic study on devotion; this is not a requirement for a devotional aspirant. Many professors can teach on the subject of devotion and draw conclusions, but they do not practice devotion in their lives.

This point can be further understood by taking the example of a professor who has some understanding of devotion, but in reality, it is only a matter of discussion for him. The professor may speak brilliantly on various subjects, but these topics have nothing to do with his own philosophies, which can be far removed from the path. Sage Narad is sharing his teachings with those who want to understand and practice devotion.

Devotion is accessible to all. Sage Shandilya mentions in his *Shandilya Bhakti Sutra* (aphorism 78), "All are eligible for the path of devotion, including those who are socially unprivileged." Lord Krishn states in the *Bhagwad Gita* (9.32), "If merchants, menial servants, people born in impious families or women[6] receive My shelter, they also attain the supreme goal." One who correctly understands and receives the teachings of the devotional scriptures like the *Narad Bhakti Sutra* becomes a vessel of Lord Krishn's grace[7] and attains release from the cycle of birth and death.

A person desiring to follow the path of devotion need not have any kind of special status in society to understand this devotional science. Old age is not a prerequisite for practicing devotion. Often, young people leave this practice by saying it is not suited to their lifestyles; especially when they have desires for money, reputation, fame, vices, and so forth. Some make an incorrect assumption and feel that they can only attain or practice devotion[8] once they are able to detach from material attachments. One does not need to renounce anything before beginning devotional practice.

In the scriptures, devotion is known as Bhakti Devi. When a child plays outside and becomes dirty, the mother does not think that her child should take a bath first and only then she can hold him. When a mother sees her child's condition, she holds him in her arms, gives

---

[6] All these are people who might have been denied access to the path if Krishn had not clearly stated otherwise.

[7] Grace means one receives something that one has not merited or something that one is not worthy of.

[8] When one attains devotion, one has a taste for devotional practice. He tries to find ways to dedicate more time in order to build his relationship with the Lord, and he yearns to associate with His devotees.

him a bath, wipes his body, combs his hair, dresses him, feeds him milk and then when he is fully ready, she gives her child to his father. In the same way, Bhakti Devi does not see castes, creeds or defects in her children. She accepts everyone, decorates them with good qualities, feeds them love, and when they are ready, she offers her children to the Lord. Therefore, one does not need to avoid devotion in life. When devotion comes, good qualities will automatically come.

Exclusive loving devotion to Lord Krishn purifies devotees of unrighteous actions, which manifest in them due to a lack of knowledge, negative influences from their upbringing and exposure to inappropriate association. Devotion alone is capable of leading such persons directly to the higher destination of the spiritual world and into the Lord's eternal association. Desires for sense enjoyment may be there, but these desires should not be strong enough to exclude the learner from the pursuit of spirituality. The scriptures describing the path of devotion are particularly helpful for a person who is neither extremely engrossed in material desires nor has he the utmost spirit of renunciation.

3. There are two main purposes (*prayojan*) of this scripture: the first aim is to guide one who is yearning to become a devotee. The *Priti Sandarbh* (section 65) says, "Devotion prepares, directs and allows the spiritual aspirant to see the Lord because the Lord is controlled by devotion only. Devotion is best of all."

The second aim is to give shelter to those aspirants who lack an understanding of sacred love because they do not have the association of elevated devotees, and therefore, they are not on the right path to reach the Lord. Some aspirants practice according to their own understanding and feel they can reach sacred love, but according to the scriptures, there is a process to reach this level of devotion.

4. What is the relationship (*sambandh*) between the subject matter and the ultimate goal to be attained for one on the path of devotion? Here, mere intellectual understanding is not enough. The teachings are based upon Sage Narad's personal experiences and supported by others, as recorded in the scriptures. Such experiences are essential to help define devotion; otherwise, people may get carried away with their own understanding, and as a result they may neglect to put into practice the true spiritual principles. Without some attraction for devotion, one cannot even begin one's spiritual journey: a journey that eventually blossoms into sacred love.

Sutra 2

|| *sā tvasmin paramapremarūpā* ||

Devotion has been described as sacred love towards the Lord.

This aphorism defines devotion. There are many scriptures that elaborate on the different classifications of devotion:

- The *Swetaswatar Upanishad* (6.23) states, "The teachings presented here will be experienced as internal revelation when received by those great souls who have great loving devotion for the *Guru*[9] and for the Lord."

- The *Bhaktirasamrtasindhu* (1.1.11) states, "The best kind of devotion is one in which the devotee constantly offers loving worship, care and service to Lord Krishn, in a way that is pleasing to Him, free from any ulterior motive and not shrouded by reliance on intellectual knowledge (*gyan*) or purposeful action (*karm*)."

- The *Narad Pancaratra* states, "Devotion is action performed for the purpose of attaining Lord Krishn. By performing these activities, one attains sacred love," and, "Devotion is service performed with the senses, free from all worldly motivation, for the Lord of the senses."

- The *Srimad Bhagwatam* (3.29.11-12) states, "Just as the current of the Ganga River flows eternally towards the ocean, similarly at the mere hearing of My glories, the heart of the devotee melts and flows in an unbroken stream towards Me. My devotee loves Me alone, without selfish desires. Such is the path of devotion."

- The *Gopal Tapini Upanishad* (2.1) states, "The meaning of devotion is to serve Him with adoration, by focusing the mind on Him, with no expectation of gain in this life or the next."

- The *Bhakti Rasayan* (1.3) states, "What is devotion? It is a state in which the heart, melted by the intensity of spiritual practice, flows constantly towards the Lord."

---

[9] A *Guru* is a spiritual master or guide.

- The *Shandilya Bhakti Sutra* (aphorism 2) states, "Devotion is unwavering attachment to the Lord."

There are ample definitions of devotion from a wealth of scriptures, but Sage Narad has revealed the essence of devotion in simple words. Devotion should not be confused with mere emotion or fanaticism, which sometimes passes for religiosity. What is the nature of sacred love? Except for sacred love (love for the Lord), all other loves are self-centred: love for siblings, parents, children, and so forth, can be egocentric in its nature. Some may deny this point and say that there are selfless relationships in this world too, for example a mother's love for her child, or a wife's love for her husband and a husband's love for his wife. To a certain extent this is correct, but if one genuinely analyses every worldly relationship, one can find elements of selfishness in them.

A mother loves her child not because he or she is a child but because he or she is *her* child. After some time, that unselfish love transforms and she starts to expect some help and care from her child. A wife loves her husband because he is *her* husband and the same is true vice versa. She does not love every married man, nor does her husband love the wives of others. This love is not pure because there is a sense of ownership. The wife or the husband will seek personal happiness, and when certain expectations, arising from this egoism, are not fulfilled, there will be discontentment between the two. These 'I', 'me' and 'mine' are always there in every material relationship. In these relations, the exchange of love cannot be unconditional. Thus, the idea of possessiveness is always there in such loves.

Sacred love for the Lord is always unselfish, and one loves Him not because He is one's own, but because He is the natural object of love. When one loves the Lord, there is an element of wanting to possess Him, and one can also, but this possession does not bind the Lord to one person. He does not belong to the individual only, even though he or she can have a personal relationship with Him. He belongs to everyone, and generally, devotees are aware of this.

The channelling of love in a one-pointed direction is devotion. There should not be two objects of love. There is only one object and this is Lord Krishn alone. The idea of sacred love cannot be described, nor is it possible to define its nature because anything that is most elementary cannot be characterised. It is like a mixture of different sweets, which only the eater can taste. Though he is experiencing the moment, he is unable to describe the flavours and sensations.

Generally, people are familiar with intense love but find it hard to capture the essence of this feeling. However, it is important to distinguish between the two loves. Sacred love is not just intense love alone because intense love that is not directed towards the Lord is impure, whereas sacred love for the Lord is pure.

One can enquire why one loves the Lord and conversely, why one loves oneself. To have love for oneself is innate. In the same way, devotees cannot help but love the Lord. Happiness for a devotee lies in offering, not in receiving. A devotee does not expect anything from the Lord. Very few reach this level of devotion. Narad explains what happens to those who start to practice devotion and fall before reaching this exalted stage of devotion:

> "If an aspirant renounces the social duties enjoined upon him, for the sake of worshipping Krishn's lotus feet, but gets diverted before attaining the goal, can any inauspiciousness befall him because of that? On the other hand, what is truly gained by a person who fulfils all the duties tradition expects of him, if he does not love the Lord?" (*Srimad Bhagwatam* 1.5.17)

If one is diverted away from service, either through some form of deviation or through death, there is no possibility of any detriment because one who has acquired a taste for devotion is not a subject of action (*karm*) and its resulting consequence, in this life or any other. Even if the devotee is selfish, he is not debarred. In the *Srimad Bhagwatam* (3.21.24), the Lord says, "My devotee's worship is never in vain."

Devotion is so sublime; only those who are on this path can understand who the Lord is and the tenets of devotion can be practiced by anyone.

Sutra 3

|| *amṛtasvarūpā ca* ||

Devotion for the Lord is also like immortal nectar.

The second aphorism describes the nature of devotion, and in the third aphorism, Narad expands on the definition. He describes the real form of devotion, which is ambrosial by nature. The *Shandilya Bhakti Sutra* states the same: "Pure devotion to the Lord makes one immortal, beatific and blissful."

There are three types of nectar in this world:

1. The churning of the ocean by the gods[10] and demons yielded ambrosia (*amrit*). This nectar is for the gods. It removes all kinds of disease, but it does not save one from the path of action attached to good acts. According to their good deeds, people go to heaven and drink this nectar and reside there until the fruits of their good actions are exhausted. Once the rewards have reduced to a certain degree, the souls come back to Earth. Devotion is not like this kind of nectar.

2. Another kind of nectar comes from the moon. It comes to Earth by moonlight, and herbs, plants and trees absorb this; it can be received by them. The moonlight causes wheat and grain to mature, gives strength to the body and removes hunger, but this nectar cannot stop disease and death. Devotion is also not this kind of nectar.

3. There is nectar which is connected to the Lord, explains Sage Narad. Only the Lord receives this nectar. Earthly love is limited by time, place and circumstance and the objects of this worldly affection, which are all impermanent. This kind of love has a beginning and an end. For this reason, ordinary love is not eternal. On the other hand, once sacred love begins, it is everlasting because it has no dependency on anything temporary. It starts from within us, and the object of love is within us too. Man constantly seeks his share of peace and happiness in this world, and since he does not know the real source of these, he searches for them in the midst of sense objects. But when he begins to understand and devote himself to the Lord, he starts to relish the nectar, which gives him supreme bliss and peace.

---

[10] According to the scriptures, there are 3.3 billion gods and goddesses who maintain nature and all the Universes and are controlled by Lord Krishn.

There are three differences between earthly love and sacred love: first of all, earthly love is temporary; second, its intensity may go so far but it will not reach the supreme state; and third, it is directed towards impermanent objects. Such qualities are not there in sacred love. To give a clear idea of what is meant by devotion, the *Srimad Bhagwatam* states, "The mind that constantly meditates on the objects of the senses unavoidably takes pleasure in their temporary joys, but the mind that constantly remembers Me, merges into Me." A devotee never craves for liberation; he always yearns to enjoy the love of the Lord and to serve Him solely for His pleasure.

Once, Lord Krishn was in a pastureland herding cows. All of a sudden, in separation, He started to cry, "Radha! Radha!"[11] This mood of longing expressed itself in a melody (*madhur sangeet*), which hypnotized the whole world. When Saraswati (the goddess of knowledge) heard the divine rhythm, she was attracted towards its origin. Saraswati came to the pastureland and witnessed the most handsome personality, Lord Krishn. She was mesmerized by Him and asked Him to accept her as His maidservant. Lord Krishn rejected Saraswati's plea. In despair, she became numb and transformed herself into a stalk of bamboo. Lord Krishn accepted the bamboo and made it His flute. Now Lord Krishn plays this very flute and enjoys the love of His devotee, Saraswati. In return, she relishes Krishn's love because she serves Him for the sake of His pleasure.

There are two things that are compulsory in devotion: *raag* (attachment) and *bhog* (offering). Attachment means glorifying the Lord's Name, His pastimes, His fame, His beauty, and so forth. *Bhog* means an offering made to the Lord during His worship for the sole purpose of His happiness, and this can be in the form of offering food and clothes to the Lord, and so forth.

Devotion means serving with love, not love alone. It can be understood in simple terms. For example, a husband returns home after work.

He asks his wife, "Could you please give me a glass of water?"

"Sweetheart, you know I love you, but I will not fetch you a glass of water," she replies. Again the husband asks, and the wife replies, "Darling, I love you but I will not fetch you a glass of water." He may get irritated because he knows that love does not only mean saying, "I love you," it also means serving the object of love.

---

[11] Radha expanded from Krishn so that He could experience and enjoy His own love, through Her love for Him. She is His Soul and His internal potency.

The *Srimad Bhagwatam* (10.47.24) highlights the same point: "Charity, vows, fire offerings, repetition of *mantras*,[12] scriptural study and other ritual acts should be done with the sole aim of attaining devotion for Lord Krishn." The following aphorism reveals how aspirants can understand real devotion.

[12] A *mantra* is a string of Sanskrit syllables or words, used in prayer, which contains the full power of the divine person (or persons) whose name it contains.

Sutra 4

|| *yallabdhvā pumān siddho bhavati amṛto bhavati tṛpto bhavati* ||

After obtaining devotion, the devotee becomes perfect, immortal and extremely satisfied.

Devotion is its own fulfilment, and after gaining this wealth, a devotee discovers an unlimited satisfaction in his devotional practice. He does not feel any emptiness thereafter. Shankaracharya states in *Shivananda Lahari*, "Let me be born as a man or a god, an animal or a tree, a bug, a worm or a bird. I care nothing for external forms as long as my heart is full of love for Your lotus feet." The first point in this aphorism says, "After obtaining devotion, the devotee becomes perfect . . . ." Once an aspirant reaches this level, he becomes calm, humble and perfect. The perfection or *siddhi*, in this context, does not mean supernatural power. Here, *siddhi* means the attainment of the Lord.

A *siddh* is one who has attained the ultimate stage of devotion for the Lord. In certain situations, *siddhi* means supernatural powers, and there are some powers that a devotee may attain as a side-effect of devotional practice, but the devotee does not yearn for this fruit. Nowadays, it is a common belief that devotion means attaining superhuman powers and people are following those persons who attain them. But it is not this *siddhi* that a devotee acquires when he obtains devotion. One who uses such powers for selfish reasons or personal gain will fall from the path of devotion.

Powers may breed arrogance in the person, which is the most dangerous obstacle in one's devotional life. He may consume most of his time in using or demonstrating his *siddhis* instead of applying himself in devotion. *Siddhi,* in the devotional context, is perfection in devotion. It is like perfectly boiled rice, which becomes soft, and after this stage it will not revert back to being hard again. In the same way, after attaining devotion a devotee becomes soft in nature and humble; arrogance due to wealth and social status, and so forth, vanishes from him. In the *Patanjali Yog Sutra*, there are eight yogic perfections such as to become extremely small, to become extremely large, to become very heavy or to acquire anything one desires, but these achievements are material; they are not perfection. Perfection means to regain the soul's true divine form and engage in devotional practice for the Lord.

Once, a spiritual master Gyandev and his disciple Naamdev were crossing a desert. After walking some distance, they felt the urge to drink water. Both were thirsty and luckily they found a well, but the rope and bucket were missing. So, the spiritual master used his superhuman powers and went inside the well, drank the water and returned. Gyandev asked his disciple Naamdev to do the same, but the disciple declined. Naamdev started to cry and said, "When a devotee of the Lord is thirsty, will the Lord not even quench his thirst?" Two teardrops fell from his eyes into the well and the water level rose higher. The disciple was able to drink the water without using any superhuman powers. Here, Naamdev is an example of a true *siddh* devotee. The aspirant should seek the association of a *siddh* like Naamdev, and not be misled in pursuit of supernatural powers (*siddhis*).

The second part of the aphorism states "the devotee becomes immortal . . . ." Immortal does not mean that the body becomes permanent. This is obviously impossible. The common conception of immortality suggests that the body becomes eternally alive. Once an attachment to his physical body completely disappears, the devotee becomes free from the fear of death. When material desires disappear, the notion of mortality ceases to be a reality and he becomes immortal. The devotee does not yearn to attain any worldly possessions, nor does he have any attachments to them; the idea of possession of objects and attachments to them can become obstacles on this path. When one drowns in the nectar of devotion, he never dies because this nectar is immortality itself. Devotion is eternal, and one who practices it also becomes eternal. The devotee is always revelling in this love, and this feeling of ecstasy can never be taken away from him.

The third part of the aphorism states "and he becomes extremely satisfied." People can have a tendency to be greedy; there can be an inclination to gain more fame and to earn more wealth, and so forth.

> A man afflicted with desire can never be satisfied, even if he has everything the world has to offer including grain, wealth, livestock and women. Indulgence of desire never satisfies desire, just as pouring butter on a fire does not put the fire out but rather makes it burn more intensely. (*Srimad Bhagwatam* 9.19.13-14)

Any sense object that one loves and enjoys will not have a lasting effect. When one is separated from the object, the feelings start to disappear. Suppose one likes the smell of a particular perfume. One will enjoy the scent whilst the fragrance remains. This feeling lasts only as long as the senses are in contact with the external object. This is not the nature of devotion. Once a devotee has acquired a taste for this devotion, nothing else that he can possibly desire compares to it. Here, Narad explains that after attaining devotion, a devotee does not yearn for anything. He becomes free from all desires. The *Bhagwad Gita* (6.22) states, "When at last he attains that ultimate joy, he understands that there is nothing more to be attained." After acquiring this bliss, devotees do not wish to perturb their satisfaction.

> One who takes shelter of the Lord attains devotion, directly experiences Him and detaches from things unrelated to Him all in the same instance, just as a hungry person achieves satisfaction, nourishment and relief from hunger simultaneously and increasingly with each bite of food he takes. Thus, those who consistently offer Him love are blessed with devotion, detachment, and enlightened understanding of the Lord and attain supreme peace. (*Srimad Bhagwatam* 11.2.42-43)

When one is in the company of a spiritual master, one finds in him or her the qualities of perfection, immortality and satisfaction. Pure devotees also exhibit the same characteristics. They do not show superhuman powers, nor do they display numerous desires.

Sutra 5

|| *yat prāpya na kiñcid vāñchati na śocati na dveṣṭi na ramate notsāhī bhavati* ||

After attaining devotion, a devotee has no desire for anything. He does not grieve or hate, nor does he delight in anything and he does not feel encouraged to do anything else.

In the modern age, people do not understand the real essence of devotion. They consider everything from a perspective of worldly desire. In simple terms, one who is completely absorbed in 'I' has no place for 'you'. Every time a person prays and asks the Lord for something material in return, his 'I' sense becomes very pronounced, therefore removing this 'I' is the first goal one should strive for. His 'I' becomes everything to him. The Lord becomes secondary to his ego. The ego creates a major problem because it separates devotees from Him. It builds a boundary around them, making them selfish, and they have no desire to share what they have with anyone. One who is egotistical and egocentric cannot relate to others or communicate well. A genuine attempt in devotional practice removes the ego consciousness.

This is not easy to put into practice, but it becomes easier if one develops a deep yearning for Krishn and understands his position as the Lord's eternal servant. The search for the Lord should bring relief from all pain and unhappiness. One should not assume that the spiritual aspirant suffers no problems in life. This is an unrealistic notion. One may feel that just because one pursues the Lord, He should remove all obstacles from the spiritual path. The Lord can certainly do this, but if He did, man would not develop strength. A muscle is made stronger by use alone. An inactive arm, hanging lifelessly to one side, becomes weak and withered. If a person wants to build his weak muscles, he has to use them regularly. Similarly, an aspirant needs to practice devotion and use his inactive muscles of faith, compassion, dedication, patience and devotion to strengthen all these undeveloped qualities in him. Without this dedicated practice, he will not change and overcome his human weaknesses and limitations.

In the *Bhagwad Gita* (12.17), Lord Krishn states, "One who neither rejoices nor hates, who neither grieves nor yearns, who renounces both sin and piety and who has devotion for Me, is dear to Me." Sage

Narad speaks of the same *Bhagwad Gita* verse in his fifth aphorism. Lord Krishn is revealing the quality of those devotees whom He dearly loves. When an aspirant attains devotion, his heart will not crave anything else. He will find complete contentment and satisfaction in the Lord. Such a man has only one prayer: that he be deluded no more by this material world.

> The Lord's personal qualities are so sweet that He attracts everyone. Sages and people who have attained constant experience of the bliss of the soul lovingly serve the Lord, without any motive but to give Him pleasure. (*Srimad Bhagwatam* 1.7.10)

In this aphorism, the first point is, "After attaining devotion . . . ." Devotion can be attained in three ways:

1. By heritage (birth into a practicing family)
2. By blessings or association of saints, godly persons or devotees
3. By practicing devotion to purify one's heart, making way for devotion to blossom within

The second point is, "a devotee has no desire for anything." Desires come from feelings of incompleteness, and grief arises when there is a loss of something one holds dear. For the person who has realised the truth, there is nothing more to be desired. He does not grieve because this devotion cannot be lost or taken away from him. Even if the devotee has to lose many things in the world, such as his family, friends and eventually his body, he will be unaffected by this because these things are nothing in comparison to what he has acquired. And so there is no grief. The devotee is eternally satisfied.

Patanjali states, "A person of discriminating intelligence understands that everything in the material world is a source of pain because even one's own thoughts result in suffering as a consequence of loss of happiness, anticipation of loss of happiness or desire for happiness." Even worldly joy is rooted in sorrow, for misery is both the cause of pleasure and its consequence. A man can expect to be free from the misery of loss, desire, ignorance and ego only after attaining devotion. Such a person is beyond both pleasure and pain, which arises from merit and demerit.

Obstacles to the attainment of objects one desires become the cause of hatred in one's mind. The *Yog Sutra* (2.8) states, "Hate is always directed towards an object or person by whom one has been hurt or injured." Vyasdev comments on this verse, "It is the nature of anger to get rid of such an offending object or person." Hate is one of the main obstacles in devotional life, though it can be removed by devotional practice. It is an impediment because a person who hates someone keeps that person in his or her thoughts constantly. A person actually loves his enemy more than his friend because the mind is focused on the enemy all the time. Much of one's energy is diverted towards animosity. Unfortunately, in human life, hatred penetrates the deeper levels within, more so than love. On the contrary, good thoughts make a devotee peaceful, balanced, happy and joyous.

Often, a beginner on the devotional path weakens himself by reacting to events that are beyond his control and events which do not always have a favourable outcome. One must develop the determination that uncontrollable situations will not cause emotional disturbances, and one needs to develop a consciousness whereby his actions will not hurt or harm others.

When an aspirant grieves due to worldly misfortunes he experiences pain and misery, but when he chants the Holy Name he revels in joy, and this blissful feeling takes him away from all the hate and miseries, ultimately connecting him to the Lord. Because he does not have any hostility towards anyone, he sees only the Lord's hand in everything, and he also witnesses that the Lord resides in all beings. If a devotee hates, it will be equal to hating the Lord Himself. Everything that comes to the devotee is only a token of His love, and regarded with such feeling, it is always welcomed by the devotee. Therefore, the devotee cannot hate when he does not bear any resentment towards anyone.

Furthermore, he does not rejoice over anything. One rejoices when some desire is satisfied or when pain or problems are removed. Such joys are temporary. The *Katha Upanishad* (2.12) states, "Upon attaining the self-effulgent Lord, the wise relinquish all mundane joy and sorrow." When a devotee attains devotion, nothing else can give him that feeling of bliss. The devotee is always immersed in joy, in which the ego is completely absent. Lastly, the devotee does not have any urges. "He who desires nothing for himself, who is wise, who is pure in mind, heart and body, who is undistracted and impartial, who is free from ego and who has devotion for Me, is very dear to Me." (*Bhagwad Gita* 12.16)

Material desires can never be completely satisfied because one desire leads to another. For example, a husband and wife build a home on a limited amount of income. They are happy with their beautiful house but they do not have money to furnish the interior. There is a desire to buy furnishings, and soon they develop desire after desire, for example to acquire more items. Once they have a family, they start to save money for their children's education and welfare, and so forth. Eventually, one is caught in the snare of desires and there is no end in sight. But a devotee who attains the Lord feels no urge to acquire material possessions.

Naturally, one may enquire about the purpose of this life. The higher practices of the devotional path may appear cold, but the absence of desire in a devotee does not imply that he is lifeless; the devotee is completely full and satisfied. When a pitcher is immersed in the ocean, it fills with water and is surrounded by water. When the filled pitcher reaches the bottom of the ocean, it becomes stable. It is not possible to imagine any movement within this pitcher (in other words a flow of water to a space where water is absent) because it is full inside and out. If the pitcher is half full, it will float on the surface and the unpredictable waves of the ocean will carry the pitcher away. And so, a devotee who is drowning in the love of the Lord becomes completely stable, and thus he remains undistracted by material desires, which are like the turbulent waves of the ocean. For this reason he does not crave for anything.

When a devotee does not wish for anything, it means he does not want for himself. He does not grieve for personal loss and at the same time, he does not enjoy or feel elated through any personal gain. It is not that the devotee invariably becomes inert like a stone. On the contrary, he serves for the sake of others, remaining free from selfishness.

Sutra 6

|| *yatjñātvā matto bhavati stabdho bhavati ātmarāmo bhavati* ||

After understanding devotion, the devotee becomes intoxicated. He becomes stunned in ecstasy and thus finds all joy in his Self.

In this aphorism, Sage Narad continues to describe the nature of a perfect devotee. Just like an alcoholic, a drug addict or a person intoxicated by any vice has no cognition of the external world, a devotee, having attained devotion, becomes completely absorbed and madly engrossed in bliss, detached from material pain and pleasure.

The *Srimad Bhagwatam* (11.2.40) states:

> By performing devotional practice consistently and chanting the Name of his beloved Krishn, the devotee attains sacred love and his heart melts. Thus he rises far above the common folk and social norms. Not for the sake of showing off, but naturally, he behaves as if mad. He loudly laughs, weeps, calls His Name and sings. Sometimes seeing his Beloved appear before his eyes, he dances to please Him.

Moreover, the *Srimad Bhagwatam* (11.3.32) reveals the symptoms:

> The hearts of such devotees attain a unique state. Sometimes they begin to worry that they have not found their Beloved. 'Who can I go to? Who will help me? Who can take me to Him?' So they start to cry. Sometimes they attain a vision of Him and they begin to laugh. Sometimes they become immersed in joy from the experience of His direct presence. Sometimes they talk to the Beloved, and sometimes they start to glorify Him. Sometimes they do not find Him nearby so they start to search, and when they find Him, they attain supreme peace and stillness in His presence.

The devotee Prahlad explains these symptoms of intoxication in the *Srimad Bhagwatam* (7.7.35-36):

> Like one affected by a malefic astrological influence, sometimes he laughs like a madman, sometimes he wails

> pitifully, sometimes he meditates, and sometimes he glorifies the Lord to others. When he is completely absorbed in Krishn, he draws long breaths and without hesitation, he calls out the Name of his Beloved. Then, by the supreme power of devotion, all his bonds are broken. Thinking about Krishn in his heart, he becomes saturated with Him. At that time the seeds of his actions are burnt and that devotee attains his Beloved.

This is the path of devotion. When a devotee attains this stage of intoxication, he does not crave to be in any situation that is not connected to his practice: in other words, any circumstance that does not serve His Lord. Therefore, the devotee's joy becomes eternal. If his bliss becomes dependent on peripheral factors disconnected to the path, the level of ecstasy he experiences will also fluctuate. Hence the joy and happiness may disappear. The joy in devotion is not controlled by anything extraneous and therefore there is no condition that limits this pleasure. This bliss is unconditional and unrestricted; hence it is uninterrupted and endless. The word *ātmarām* in the Sanskrit version of the aphorism indicates the same mood: a mood where a devotee is completely absorbed in the joy of his realisation of the Lord.

When Chaitanya Mahaprabhu[13] went to Vrindavan,[14] Vrindavan was an undeveloped forest. A guide showed him all the locations of the pastimes of Radha and Krishn. The guide took Mahaprabhu to the places where Lord Krishn ate butter, stole the *gopis'*[15] dresses, danced with the *gopis*, and so forth. By seeing these places and hearing their glorifications, Chaitanya Mahaprabhu started to dance like a madman and rolled around in the dust of Vrindavan. The guide felt uneasy with the sight of Mahaprabhu behaving like a crazy person. Pure devotion makes a devotee crazy in love and uninhibited in the expression of his affection for the Lord.

A devotee revels in happiness as well in melancholy. One who embodies this mood is a perfect candidate for devotion. The *gopis* were happy to experience a lifetime of sadness if being in this state pleased Lord Krishn. When the *gopis* used to serve Lord Krishn, they were overjoyed with bliss and they wondered if their personal

---

[13] Chaitanya Mahaprabhu appeared on Earth in 1486 (just over 500 years ago) as the joint incarnation of Radha and Krishn.

[14] Vrindavan (150 km from New Delhi) is the equivalent of the spiritual abode (the eternal home of Radha and Krishn) on Earth. Five thousand years ago, Radha and Krishn enjoyed Their childhood pastimes in Vrindavan.

[15] *Gopis* are cowherd girls of Vrindavan and Radha is the Queen of the *gopis*.

experience of His ecstasy inflicted any pain on Him. The *gopis* spoke the following words to Lord Krishn in the *Srimad Bhagwatam* (10.31.19):

> Oh Beloved! Your lotus feet are so tender and our breasts are hard. Thus we place Your feet on our breasts extremely gently, fearing we may hurt them. You are life itself for us! The thought of Your soft lotus feet walking bare on the path at night, vulnerable to injury by sharp stones, fills us with constant anxiety.

As the devotee immerses himself in a mood where he attaches his happiness and joy in giving, the feeling transforms into love for the Lord, a love which only gives and has no desire for receiving.

2

Means to Attain Devotion

Sutra 7

|| *sā na kāmayamānā nirodharūpatvāt* ||

There is no question of *kaam* (lust/desire) in devotion because devotion is attained through complete control of the senses.

All of the preceding aphorisms stated the requirements needed by the spiritual aspirant to practice devotion. Now, Sage Narad elaborates on the requirements one needs to receive devotion. This aphorism talks about controlling one's senses from *kaam,* and in Sanskrit, *kaam* has two meanings: lust or desire. The word desire encompasses all wants, whereas lust describes a particular type of desire. Different commentators have interpreted this *kaam* according to their understanding. But it is not clear whether Sage Narad spoke of desire or lust; therefore this commentary will aspire to capture both moods.

Nowadays, the word love is readily misunderstood. People tell their partners, parents and siblings that they love them, without honouring the sanctity of such a powerful emotion. In the name of loving someone, a person can wound their lover's heart and mind, whilst in their absence resenting and criticizing them to others. Another serious problem is possessiveness, which breeds hatred or fear towards others. This is why the lover cannot enjoy life; he becomes insecure and possessive of those he claims to love. Love teaches one to respect people. Love is not a spontaneous or a sensual feeling one feels for someone. This is not love; it is a short-lived emotion. Love is understanding; it is giving. When one loves, one offers unconditionally without expecting anything in return. Expectations are the root of all problems in life. But the *Chaitanya Charitamrit* (1.4.165) states, "Lust is the desire to please one's own senses, while love is the desire to offer pleasure to Krishn's senses."

If one has love that is devoid of expectations and without lust, one can attain the Lord. Here, Sage Narad stresses that lust is the greatest obstacle because lust manifests in the mind. There are four urges: food, sex, sleep, and self-preservation, which are the root causes of all emotions. Food is a necessity of the body first and then of the mind. Sex is a necessity of the mind first and then it is expressed through the body. When lust keeps the mind busy, a devotee cannot meditate on the Lord. In the book *For a Future to Be Possible: Commentaries on the Five Wonderful Precepts* (1993), Thich Nhat Hanh writes:

> A sexual relationship may be an act of deep communication between body and spirit. This is a very important encounter, not to be done in a casual manner. You know that in your soul there are certain areas – memories, pain, secrets – that are private, that you would only share with the person you love and trust the most. You do not open your heart and show it to just anyone. In the Imperial City, there is a zone you cannot approach called the Forbidden City; only the king and his family are permitted to circulate there. There is a place in your soul like that that you do not allow anyone to approach except the one you love and trust the most.

Casual sex cannot be called love because love is deep, beautiful, and whole. In sexual relationships, respect is one of the most important elements and sexual union should be like an important rite, a ritual performed with mindfulness as well as great respect, care and love. If some form of desire motivates someone, then this is not love. Desire for one's own physical satisfaction is not love. When Sage Narad discusses *kaam*, he asks the aspirant to restrain his senses from desires. An important quality of a devotee is that he tries to please the Lord by his devotion.

The following tale illustrates how a person tries to help others to control their desires but neglects to constrain his own wants. There was a man who made *chapatis* (Indian flat bread) for himself and he applied a good amount of oil to them. But when he made *chapatis* for the saints and beggars, he never used any oil. He thought that saints are renounced and by giving them oily *chapatis*, their desire would increase. He believed that only those who are not renounced are free to enjoy taste. An attitude where one tries to control others without restraining one's own senses is not beneficial. Saints have renounced because they are able to control their senses. In order to attain devotion, those who are unable to manage their desires should try to control their own senses. But when a devotee has one-pointedness in devotion, all desires are completely eliminated.

A person can have endless desires and he is not always able to control how fast these cravings grow. One usually prays to the Lord to have something that one cannot get, or that one finds difficult to acquire by one's own efforts. The desire may be wealth, a material object that one would like to possess, fame, and so forth. This is human nature. This demanding devotion is not the type of devotion that Sage Narad speaks of. In this aphorism, the nature of devotion is pure and cannot be attached to any kind of desire because the very nature of the process to attain pure love negates any form of worldly desire.

The *Bhagwad Gita* mentions four types of devotees:

1. *Aarta*: The one who is in trouble
2. *Jigyasu*: The one who is inquisitive and desires to know the mystery of the Universe
3. *Artharthi*: The one who desires material benefit
4. *Gyani*: The one who is knowledgeable and knows that the Lord is the only object worth attaining

Narad asks the aspirant to control his senses, and in the *Bhagwad Gita*, it appears that Lord Krishn is stating the opposite, "Those who have desire are My devotees." Both are correct and not contrasting. In this quote, the Lord is saying that His devotees are also those who come to Him asking for their desires to be fulfilled by Him. At the same time, Sage Narad is not asking one to suppress those desires, but he advises one to control them and use them for the pursuit of eternal bliss. The *Srimad Bhagwatam* (10.14.36) states, "Until one becomes Yours, his material desires are like thieves, his home is like a prison, and attachment binds him like shackles on his feet."

Usually, aspirants are attracted towards devotion because they want to fulfil their desires. When a devotee practices devotion, he can attain supernatural powers, which draws others to him. Therefore, the devotee obtains fame and respect, which may divert him towards distractions unfavourable to the path of devotion, creating obstacles in his progress, even to the point where he is unable to attain the Lord. Devotees who want to achieve the real goal of devotion should carefully guard against all these material desires and stay close to the devotional path with humility and detachment. Devotees ask the Lord for devotion only. The following quotes give examples of this:

Prahlad asks the Lord, "Oh great Giver! If You wish to give me something, I pray for this blessing: may the seed of desire never sprout within my heart." (*Srimad Bhagwatam* 7.10.7)

One day Arjun, the great warrior and dearest friend of Krishn, asked Him, "Why do You always praise the *gopis* so much? If anyone speaks of love, You immediately start to sing their praises. What is so special about their love that sets it apart from the love of others?"

"The *gopis* cleanse, perfume and decorate their bodies only for the sake of pleasing Me, and not for any other reason. Is there anyone else in the Universe who has love like theirs?" Lord Krishn replied.

The *Srimad Bhagwatam* (10.10.38) describes what aspirants need to do to attain this level of devotion:

> May our speech always glorify You, may our ears always hear Your sweet stories, may our hands always serve You, and may our hearts delight in the remembrance of Your lotus feet. The whole Universe is Your residence. May our heads always bow before all. The saints are Your own body. May our eyes always behold them.

By adopting this frame of mind, one starts to attain devotion. A saintly woman, Shabri, used to sweep the road everyday with the hope that one day the Lord would cross her path. The actions and fruits of this loving devotion were for the sake of the Lord's happiness and not for personal happiness. Therefore, in devotion one should practice with this mood. Devotion itself is the goal, and such desire is not called desire because devotion itself takes the aspirant away from desire.

Sutra 8

|| *nirodhastu lokavedavyāpāranyāsaḥ* ||

Control or cessation means to give up all kinds of social customs and religious rituals governed by *Vedic* injunction.

Offering all kinds of social and religious rituals to Lord Krishn is known as cessation or abstention. Lord Krishn states in the *Bhagwad Gita* (9.27-28):

> All that you do, all that you eat, all that you offer in the sacred fire, all that you give, all that you endure: do all this as an offering to Me. By doing so, you will become free from the good and bad results of your actions and you will attain Me.

In his commentary on the abovementioned verses, the great saint Nimbarkacharya states:

> The connection between Lord Krishn and His devotees is of the sweetest nature, where the Creator and Controller of all that exists unconditionally accepts and takes pleasure in the simplest offerings – a fruit, a flower, a leaf or water – if offered to Him with love. A devotee qualifies when he offers everything he performs in his daily life to Lord Krishn, such as the rites and rituals (according to the scriptures), including each prayer and whatever he eats, surrendering himself completely to the Lord. The devotee understands that the Lord is the Master of the entire creation and the only One who rewards the fruits of every single action performed in every lifetime, including the present. The devotee devotes himself exclusively with one-pointedness, renouncing the worldly objects, which bind the individual consciousness to the material world, in exchange for the nectar of communion with the Lord. Thus, he achieves liberation from the fruits of his actions both good and bad. Surrendering the rewards of such deeds negates the power of actions, which the material world is subjected to. Eliminating the reactive aspect of deeds, the devotee is released from the never-ending wheel of birth and death, and he ultimately attains the eternal association of Lord Krishn in His everlasting spiritual abode.

In the present age, many people do not practice such devotion because of ego consciousness. Some people pray in a temple and offer small pocket change to the Lord and ask for wishes worth millions. This attitude does not help an aspirant on the path of devotion.

One aspect separates devotees from those who do not practice devotion. A man of the Lord believes he is a soul who is part and parcel of the Lord, and he works to return to Him. On the other hand, a person who is a non-devotee thinks he is the body and does everything to please his body.

If a person asks, "Who are you?" one replies with one's given name: "I am Alexander," or, "I am Shyam." Often the confusion that arises within people is this "I." If one tries to understand the deep nature of this enquiry, one discovers that one is not Alex, Shyam, and so forth, because such names are given by one's parents and elders, and they identify the body alone, not the soul. If a name is given to the body after birth, one needs to question whether one's true nature is the body or the soul.

As long as the soul is in the body, this body is considered to be auspicious, but when the soul leaves, the body becomes inauspicious. The idea of pleasing the body is very conditional; when the body is healthy, one is physically content and when there is pain, one experiences much frustration physically. Eventually, one loses affection for a body in this condition. What one actually loves is the happiness and peace within, not the physical shell itself and this feeling of bliss can come when a person starts to obtain devotion in his life.

Devotion always gives supreme happiness and supreme peace. This blissful state can be achieved once the mind is fixed and meditating on the Lord. In this situation, it becomes impossible for one to be involved in duties prescribed either by the scriptures or by society. The devotee becomes unfit for carrying out these duties. The mind and heart, which start to surrender themselves for the purpose of devotion, get absorbed in the Lord.

This can be understood through a simple story taken from a few verses in the *Srimad Bhagwatam* (10.29). Lord Krishn played His flute, and the *gopis* immediately left what they were doing in order to meet Him. To test them, Lord Krishn asked:

> Why have you come here in the dark night and in this deep forest? All of you have left your houses without asking anyone's permission. Society will criticize you and find fault with you. You should have remained loyal and engaged in household duties. Instead, you have neglected your duties as faithful women, which is condemnable. Also, in this deep forest there are so many wild animals, it will be dangerous for you to stay here. So go back and keep yourselves engaged in your duties.

The *gopis* replied, "Our minds and actions were fully engaged in our household duties, but since You, the only Goal of our soul, stole our minds, our hands have lost their power to do chores and our feet have lost the ability to move. Therefore, how shall we return now? What shall we do there if we go back?"

In simple terms, when a person comes to the stage of pure devotion, he knows that he does not belong to anyone other than the Lord.

Sutra 9

|| *tasminnananyatā tadvirodhiṣūdāsīnatā ca* ||

In devotion there is cessation of everything other than one-pointedness to the Lord and indifference to things opposed to Him.

One who serves the Lord is taken care of by Him. In an attempt to give up social and religious activities opposed to devotion, the mind needs to make adjustments. This aphorism states that total absorption in the Lord and one-pointedness for Him is required from the devotee, and in return, the Lord will take care of him.

Often, the spiritual aspirant will get frustrated in life and he may not care for the objects of enjoyment, which are material in nature. This is not real renunciation, as the mind is not absorbed in the Lord. The correct meaning of renunciation is detachment from worldly desire and attachment to Him. If the mind is partially absorbed in the Lord and partially in the material world, the mind's flow towards Him will be obstructed. One needs to direct one's mind single-mindedly towards the Lord, and the mind should have complete indifference towards material objects. This meditation is the only factor needed for attainment of God-realisation. In the *Bhagwad Gita* (9.22), Lord Krishn promises the same:

> *ananyāścintayanto māṁ ye janaḥ paryupāsate*
> *teṣām nityābhiyuktānāṁ yogakṣemam vahāmyaham*
>
> "I personally take care of My devotees who constantly think about Me and nothing else. I conserve what they have and I carry to them what they do not have."

In this verse, the word *ananyāś* means exclusivity. Exclusive denotes such devotees who have no other goal than the Lord. In his commentary on this *Bhagwad Gita* verse, Keshav Kashmiri states:

> This means thinking of nothing but constantly serving Him with one's whole heart and soul. Because of the all-encompassing nature of their devotion, they sometimes forget to take care of their own physical, sensory and mental needs. In this case, the Lord Himself arranges for their care, supplying all the necessities they need for their existence.

> He protects them in all respects from any situation that may obstruct them from attaining Him in this very life.

Once, a devotee named Jagannath Mishra was writing a commentary on the same *Bhagwad Gita* verse (9.22). He felt that a devotee is a servant to his Master (the Lord). Therefore, the Master taking care of His servant seemed inappropriate to Jagannath. He felt this was a mistake, and so he crossed out the word *vahāmyaham* (I carry) and changed it into *dadāmyaham* (I supply). He was aware that there were no vegetables or spices left in the house, but he had no money. Leaving for his daily bath in the ocean, Jagannath Mishra decided that upon his return home, he would try to find a way to purchase the necessary items so that his family would not go hungry.

Meanwhile, a small boy came to Jagannath's house, carrying a basket of vegetables and spices. Jagannath's wife asked, "Who are you? Why have you come here?"

"My grandmother likes your husband's discourses very much, so she sent this gift for you," the child replied.

Jagannath Mishra's wife saw bruises and marks on this small boy's beautiful face and asked him what had happened.

The boy explained, "I saw your husband and tried to give him this gift, but he scratched me badly and told me to bring it to you instead."

At the thought of this violent act, Jagannath's wife became unhappy and angry. Upon Jagannath's return home, his wife confronted him and asked what made him harm the boy.

A surprised Jagannath protested, "I did not go to market, nor did I meet or beat any boy."

Pondering over this confusion, Jagannath realised that this boy must be none other than the Lord Himself, who came to make Jagannath see that He is always there to help His devotees. The Lord carries to them what they lack, whilst preserving what they already have. By changing the word *vahāmyaham* (I carry) into *dadāmyaham* (I supply), Lord Krishn felt that Jagannath Mishra had disregarded the truth as spoken by Him, hence the boy appeared with scratches on his face, a physical metaphor for Jagannath crossing the Lord's words out in the *Bhagwad Gita* verse. With his faith restored, Jagannath changed the verse back to its original form.

Saint Tulsi Das lived in a hut in Varanasi. A thief came to steal from Tulsi Das' hut, but he found two warriors armed with bows and arrows guarding his abode. That night, the thief returned again and again to find an opportunity to escape those guards, but each time he came, he found both guards extremely attractive and mesmerising.

In the morning, the thief fell at the feet of Tulsi Das and told him, "I do not want anything from you. I just want to see those two beautiful guards again."

After hearing the descriptions of those guards, who were none other than Lord Ram and His brother Lakshman, Tulsi Das thought, "This must be the work of my Lord because I do not have any guards. I have collected some objects for my living, and as a result, my Lord had to trouble Himself and personally come here in the night, disturbing His own sleep, just to protect me." Tulsi Das took all of his belongings and distributed them to beggars because he did not want to disturb His Lord again.

A true devotee does not want anything from the Lord. He does not even want that the Lord should waste His precious and valuable time on him. After achieving this level of devotion, the aphorism states "indifference to things opposed to Him." One should avoid people and objects that oppose one's devotion. These objects are there to tempt a devotee away from his path. When a person is arguing, he is not able to perform his devotional practice at that time and his mind becomes troubled. Devotees who are unstable will be questioned on their devotion and their spiritual master's teachings may be criticized too. The devotee will draw negativity to himself, which will not allow him to enjoy the peace and happiness that he wants. The aim is to avoid such troublesome situations and enjoy devotional practice without interruption.

Sutra 10

|| *anyāśrayāṇāṁ tyāgo'nanyatā* ||

Discarding everything except the Lord is one-pointedness in devotion.

In the *Bhagwad Gita* (8.14), Lord Krishn advises Arjun, "He who remembers Me constantly and single-mindedly attains Me easily." The Lord is not impossible to attain, and He is there for all those who are lovingly devoted to Him. Furthermore, He Himself is unable to bear any separation from His devotees for any length of time. Lord Krishn's divine nature is such that He can be accessed only by devotion and by no other method. Various scriptures confirm that the Lord can be revealed only through loving devotion. The *Katha Upanishad* (1.2.7) states, "The Lord, even when heard about, cannot be understood without loving devotion." And also, from the *Katha Upanishad* (1.2.23), "The Lord is not attainable by instruction or by intellect." Thus, it is absolute; only devotion can attract Him and only devotion can reveal Him. This aphorism guides one to the path of devotion, which is the assured way to attain the Lord. In the *Bhagwad Gita* (9.30), Lord Krishn says:

apicet sudurācāro bhajate mām ananyabhāk
sādhureva sa mantavyaḥ samyag vyavasito hi saḥ

> "If someone worships Me single-mindedly, even if he commits sins, he should be considered a divine person for the sake of that sacred commitment."

In his commentary on this verse, Vishwanath Chakarvarti Thakur explains:

> Krishn speaks this verse to reveal His natural and spontaneous affection for His devotees and to illustrate that He does not abandon them even if they do something very wrong. Instead of abandoning His devotees when they make mistakes, He brings them away from those sins and uplifts them.

If one should ask what kinds of devotees are worthy of such treatment, the Lord says, "One who worships Me with undivided commitment." This means they do not worship any other gods or take shelter of the paths of action, knowledge and disciplined contemplation, nor do they desire anything other than Lord Krishn. It is important to note that this *Bhagwad Gita* verse does not excuse sinful acts in any way. Instead, it praises exclusive devotion. It is generally impossible for evil desires to exist within the heart of an exclusive devotee. The Sanskrit version of this *Bhagwad Gita* verse gives the depth and real meaning of a devotee who commits sinful acts. The word *api* has been used at the beginning of this verse to underline the very uncharacteristic or unintentional nature of such sinful action on the part of a devotee: in other words, those sins which have been committed unintentionally. Such misadventures may come as the result of the conditioning from a previous life or from bad association, but sinful tendencies cannot last long due to Bhakti Devi's blessings.

The very presence of devotion burns the devotee's heart in the fire of repentance and very quickly purifies it. Therefore, in the *Bhagwad Gita* (9.31), the Lord proclaims, "That devotee soon becomes sinless and attains eternal peace. Know without a doubt that one who loves Me is never destroyed." In conclusion, those who commit offences without repentance are not the devotees Lord Krishn speaks of in these two verses, but rather He speaks of those devotees who unintentionally offend. One should not misunderstand the essence of the *Bhagwad Gita* verses 9.30 and 9.31.

Despite being afflicted by lust and other material cravings, which are considered weaknesses on this path of devotion, one can still enter the devotional path. The *Srimad Bhagwatam* (10.33.40) mentions, "Whoever tells or listens to the story of Lord Krishn's loving play with the cowherd women again and again, attains the highest devotion for His lotus feet. They are quickly and eternally cured of the heart's disease, which is desire."

People usually believe that one's heart should be first cleansed of its impurities before one is able to attain the highest form of devotion, but this quote reveals that hearing or describing the pastimes of Lord Krishn with the women of Vraj[16] is a supremely powerful spiritual activity and cleansing in itself. Sensual enjoyment always distracts the mind of a devotee and makes it difficult for him to focus on devotion. The aspiring devotee may feel that desire for the sense objects, which keeps a distance between the Lord and him, is forcibly pulling him towards them and weakening his interest in devotion. The devotee must therefore take exclusive shelter of

---

[16] Vraj was a state in India over 5000 years ago. Lord Krishn was born and brought up in Vraj.

Bhakti Devi and the Lord and give up sense enjoyment. When the devotee tries to give up sense pleasure, he is unable to do so due to many layers of his conditioning. This situation is described by the Lord in His teachings to Uddhav in the *Srimad Bhagwatam* (11.20.27-28):

> An aspirant who is no longer interested in acting for the sake of personal gain and is in fact saddened by doing so, who has faith in My stories, and who knows that indulgence in sensory pleasures and desires for them lead to pain even if he cannot always give them up, should fulfil those desires when they arise. But with purity in his heart, he should remember them as the source of pain, and he should think himself greatly unfortunate for giving in to them. Simultaneously, to overcome this confused condition, he should worship Me with love and firm conviction.

A devotee who struggles with his senses demonstrates the inner conflict described in this verse. In the midst of his turmoil, the devotee sometimes gains victory and sometimes suffers defeat, but ultimately he remains firm in his inner commitment. Sage Narad highlights that this commitment is none other than meditation or one-pointed devotion towards the Lord.

Sutra 11

|| *lokavedeṣu tadanukūlācaraṇaṁ tadvirodhiṣūdāsīnatā* ||

To accept only those activities of social custom and *Vedic* injunction that are favourable to devotion and to have complete indifference towards all actions which obstruct the path to the Lord.

According to the scriptures, there are four types of actions:

1. *Nitya*: The action one performs daily
2. *Naimittik*: The action one performs according to instructions
3. *Kamya*: The action one performs to fulfil one's desires
4. *Nishid*: The action one performs that is prohibited

In this aphorism, only *nitya* and *naimittik* are prescribed and within these actions, only those activities which are favourable to the practice of devotion are recommended.

The *Bhaktirasamrtasindhu* (1.2.153) states, "May my heart always rejoice in You, just as young women rejoice in the company of young men and young men rejoice in the company of young women." When a young boy falls in love with a girl, in his craze, he is constantly distracted with thoughts of her, and his actions are directed towards pleasing her only. In the same way, this aphorism is saying that when a person is inclined towards devotion, he should accept only the activities of society and *Vedic* injunctions that are in favour of pleasing his Lord.

Sutra 12

|| *bhavatu niścayadārḍhyādūrdhvaṁ śāstrarakṣaṇam* ||

One must continue to follow scriptural injunctions until one's faith is firmly established.

One should follow the injunctions from the scriptures until firm faith is established. The *Srimad Bhagwatam* (11.20.9) supports this: "One only needs to perform the social duties prescribed in the scriptures until one gets detachment from the fruits of the actions, or until one develops firm and exclusive faith in hearing stories about Me, the singing of My Holy Name, and so forth."

Just as a man who falls in love starts to learn the likes and dislikes of his lover, in the same way, the injunctions describe the likes and dislikes of Lord Krishn. "Make the scriptures your guide and learn what should and should not be done. Understand what the scriptures reveal, and act according to their instructions." (*Bhagwad Gita* 16.24)

Sutra 13

|| *anyathā pātityaśaṅkayā* ||

Otherwise there is every possibility of falling from the ideal.

"A person who throws out all the rules of scripture and simply does whatever he wants, does not attain perfection, the supreme goal or even worldly happiness." (*Bhagwad Gita* 16.23)

To reach that level of blissful love mentioned in the previous aphorism, the aspirant should be cautious not to act according to his own emotional impulses, which may disagree with or divert him from the principles in the scripture. The regulations within the scriptures describe devotion to the Lord and are therefore non-different from Him. They are not really regulations as such; they are the Lord's likes and dislikes. One may question why He would have likes and dislikes when He is the Creator of everything and everything belongs to Him.

This can be understood in a simple way by the example of a father who has two sons, where one is good in nature and the other is not. The father will be pleased by the actions of the pleasant-natured son who strives to carve a rightful path for himself, and he will not appreciate the negative consequences of inappropriate behaviour from the second son because the father is aware that improper actions will lead him to a life of misery. He does not necessarily exclude the second child from the family just because he is difficult. Instead, the father endeavours to guide his son in the best way that he can.

In the same way, the Lord never abandons His children who may tread the wrong path, nor is He pleased if His children participate in those actions which have negative results. The Lord wishes that His progeny spread love among each other and strengthen the bond within the universal family (the world).

Therefore, to progress faster in the devotional world, some guidelines have been given in the scriptures. These are essential for devotees to learn and practice. In the *Chaitanya Charitamrit* (2.19.157), Chaitanya Mahaprabhu says that devotion is a vine (a climbing plant) and, "To prevent the powerful elephant of offences from entering, the gardener[17] must protect the vine by fencing it all around." A vine usually grows by the support of a tree. By nature,

---

[17] The gardener is an analogy for a devotee.

this plant is very fragile. But in the abovementioned verse, Chaitanya Mahaprabhu says that offences[18] are like a mad elephant. With minimal effort, a mad elephant can uproot trees in a forest, and in the face of such brutal force, the delicate vine of devotion has no means to defend herself.

The scriptures mention a few of the offences such as harming *Vaishnavs*[19] with one's thoughts or actions, blasphemy of the Holy Name and offences caused during worship of the Lord. As the aspirant takes his first step on the path of devotion, he must avoid these powerful offences because they can destroy the devotional vine in his life. One should take the instructions in the scriptures as guidelines and faithfully continue onwards on one's journey.

To illustrate this point, when a person learns to drive a car, he receives a manual highlighting the codes of conduct of driving. In the beginning, whilst he takes driving lessons, he tries to adhere to each and every rule, with the hope of becoming a better driver. But when he passes his driving test, he drives his car without the same level of attentiveness that was required as a learner.

The *Srimad Bhagwatam* (11.2.34-35) says, "Even those who are uneducated can easily come to know the Lord by practicing the method that He Himself has prescribed. This method is known as *bhagwat-dharm* or the path of devotional practice. One who accepts this path is never confused. He will not trip or fall down even if he runs with his eyes shut."

When the devotee runs with his eyes shut, it does not imply that he is blind. In his enthusiam to reach the destination, he may overlook or omit the simpler practices, to maintain the momentum in his sprint. By following the instructions in the scriptures and reaching a certain level in his devotion, he is aware of what can be overlooked without harming his practice. He does not even look back, and he runs so fast that his feet touch only parts of the path.

One who is a beginner (learner) takes every step with great care, carefully treading every part of the path and adhering to all

---

[18] Offences here are different from sins. They consist of specific acts that are listed in the scriptures, such as criticizing or harming a devotee, blasphemy of the Holy Name, and so forth. Sins can have serious physical, emotional or psychological consequences, but they do not end one's devotion for the Lord. Conversely, offences can damage or destroy one's spiritual progress. Offences lead to more offences, and one who commits them will find him or herself becoming more and more atheistic.

[19] *Vaishnavs* are devotees of Lord Vishnu/Krishn.

regulations along the way (just like the learner driver). Therefore, to nourish and strengthen the vine of devotion, Sage Narad tells the devotee to win the heart of the Lord by pleasing Him according to the guidelines stated in the scriptures.

Sutra 14

|| *loko'pi tāvadeva bhojanādivyāpārastvāśarīradhāraṇāvadhi* ||

Social activities, such as eating, should be followed and continued as long as the body lasts.

In devotional practice, one should not become so engrossed in the practice that one causes harm to one's body. A healthy body can keep the mind stable. Natural activities like sleeping, eating, exercise, and so forth, should be continued as long as body lasts. Nowadays, *yog*[20] has become a business and people are practicing to become more flexible, healthy and stress free. In ancient times, the body was seen as an instrument to perform devotion, and the primary reason for keeping the body healthy was to prevent disturbance in one's spiritual practice. Therefore, all necessary steps should be taken to maintain the body. If one ignores the body and neglects observation of certain physical conditions, the body will become diseased or weak due to this lack of care. Eventually, devotional life will also suffer because an unhealthy body will not allow one to concentrate completely.

The scriptures say, "A devotee should care for his or her body just as a concubine cares for hers, knowing that her livelihood depends on her physical condition. Similarly, if a devotee's body is weakened by illness, his spiritual practice also suffers." This body is an instrument, a vehicle for the soul to return back to the Lord. Often devotees perform excessive fasting or indulge in eating junk food. This behaviour can result in many problems. If the body becomes imbalanced by not eating enough or eating too much of the wrong foods, there is a risk of both emotional and physical disharmony. If one does not have a proper balanced diet, the body itself will demand a change. Also, those who live with chronic conditions such as diabetes have to adhere to strict eating habits and times. They should take care not to ignore the demands of the body in favour of devotional practice. Not paying attention to the needs of the body can worsen the symptoms, which can be dangerous for their health.

There is no general rule for maintaining a healthy body. For example, three people who drink a glass of wine can have different reactions, such as feeling sleepy, feeling hyperactive or vomiting, even if all of

[20] *Yog* is the Hindi word for yoga, and here the physical yoga is being discussed.

them drink the same wine and the same amount. In the same way, one must practice devotion in a way that is suitable to one's nature or bodily constitution. Ultimately, the state of a devotee's health will affect his spiritual life. A devotee considers the Lord the proprietor of his body and mind, and he only uses these objects for the purpose of devotion. After attaining the devotional path, a devotee does not misuse his body and mind for the sake of his own happiness, nor does he feel these objects should be distracted by society where he maintains his bodily relationships, such as those with his mother, father and the rest of his family.

3

The Essence of Devotion

Sutra 15

|| *tallakṣaṇāni vācyante nānāmatabhedāt* ||

Now the characteristics of devotion will be stated according to various authoritative opinions.

Many commentators have suggested that Sage Narad begins to define devotion in this aphorism by referencing the explanations given by other great sages. Yet Sage Narad has already stated the characteristics of devotion in the second and third aphorisms, namely, an aspirant should have one-pointed meditation towards the Lord and he should engage in devotional practices. He also describes the need for a devotee to feel indifference to objects that are opposed to devotion. Again, the attributes are described at great length in the seventh aphorism. The process of writing aphorisms is precise; there is no margin for ambiguity and there is no repetition of what has already been illustrated. Therefore, in this aphorism, Narad states the characteristics of devotion as described by different sages as a comparison to his own opinion.

In the previous aphorism, the effect on three people drinking the same glass of wine was given as an example, which showed how three individuals exposed to the same conditions had different symptoms. Description is an intellectual process and good quality description will depend on fine observation, clear analysis, satisfactory expression, reliability in the observer, and so forth. No two minds are alike, and this reason alone leads to different descriptions of the same experience.

> Just as the current of the Ganga River flows eternally towards the ocean, similarly, at the mere hearing of My glories, the heart of the devotee melts and flows in an unbroken stream towards Me. My devotee loves Me alone, without selfish desires. Such is the path of devotion. (*Srimad Bhagwatam* 3.29.11-12)

In the *Vishnu Puran*, Prahlad said, "The affection that the indiscriminate bear towards worldly pleasure should be redirected towards the Lord and thus transformed into devotion for Him." Ramanujacharya in the *Sribhasya* (1.1.1) comments, "Devotion is a constant flow of love, which becomes greater than one's love for oneself and is neither hindered nor diverted from its course, despite many obstacles and difficulties. It is preceded by understanding of the Lord's unparalleled and limitless excellences."

The different viewpoints of several practitioners and exponents of devotion are being described in this aphorism. Numerous teachers give various definitions of devotion, and all of them are useful in clarifying aspects of the practice. Sage Narad mentions the views of Sages Vyasdev, Garg and Shandilya in the next aphorisms.

Sutra 16

|| *pūjādiṣvanurāga iti pārāśaryaḥ* ||

According to Vyasdev, the son of Sage Parashar, devotion means attraction to worship.

Vyasdev is the compiler of the *Veds* and *Purans*. Here, he describes devotion as *puja* (worship) and *anuraag* (loving attatchment). These refer to worship of the Lord performed with sincere love and attachment. According to the scriptures of devotion, *anuraag* is loving attachment that blossoms after realisation of the Lord, when His divinity and glory are acknowledged. If an aspirant is being ignorant, in other words, if he is aware that devotion to the Lord is his goal in life but he lacks serious commitment for devotional practice and is not attached to worship, the worship becomes ritualistic. Kapil, who is an incarnation of the Lord, supports this point in the following dialogue from the *Srimad Bhagavatam* (3.29.24): "My dear mother, I am never pleased by a person who disrespects other souls, though he may worship Me with the finest accessories."

In the Sanskrit version of this aphorism, the word *puja* includes many activities such as *maansik* worship or worshipping with the mind but the word *puja* specifically refers to the worship of a Deity.[21] There is a belief that formal worship[22] is only characteristic of the first stage of devotion. But Sage Narad quotes Vyasdev's definition to show that worship can be continued even after one has attained realisation of the Lord. Great persons such as Chaitanya Mahaprabhu, Madhavacharya, Ramanujacharya and Shankaracharya performed their *puja* even after realisation of the Lord. Deity worship is a devotional practice of the utmost importance because the devotees actually experience the Lord, in other words, the Deity becomes alive.

If a devotee has committed sin, the scriptures say that Deity worship can absolve this if one is genuinely repentant and the worship is performed with love. Without love, even if one worships the Lord every day, it becomes a duty or a task. Love creates a connection

---

[21] A Deity is a two or three dimensional image, where the images are non-different from the Lord and the worship of these images, by sincere devotees, is accepted by Him. Specific ancient hymns are recited to ask Him to come and reside in those images, for the purpose of this worship.

[22] Both formal worship and veneration in this aphorism refer to Deity worship.

with the object of love, and this bond forms the closeness wherein a lover understands the mood of his beloved. Loving attachment gives fresh inspiration to love the Lord.

If worship becomes a duty, then there is no loving attachment with the service. When attachment and enjoyment are present in the worship of the Deity, a devotee can feel a connection with that Deity; he is able to sense if his Lord is hungry or craving a particular dish on that day and whether He liked the clothes He was dressed in. In such a way, a devotee can enjoy the process of worship.

Sutra 17

|| *kathādiṣviti gargaḥ* ||

According to Sage Garg, devotion is a real fondness for hearing the Lord's glories.

According to Sage Garg, devotion is a partiality for the pastimes of the Lord in the form of His Holy Name, His characteristics, His life history, prayers, composition of hymns and songs, and so forth. One's love increases when one hears the glorification of one's Lord in the stories of His divine play.

The *Srimad Bhagwatam* (11.3.31) states, "Lord Krishn destroys all sins in a fraction of a second. By remembering and helping others to remember the Lord, devotees develop sacred love and the resulting physical ecstatic reactions such as bodily hair standing on end." It is necessary for one to feel this devotion, attachment or love for the Lord's pastimes. The experience is similar to the feeling one feels when one hears his lover's good qualities. The minds and hearts of devotees discussing His divine qualities and characteristics amongst each other, reciting whatever knowledge they have of Him, whether it is great or small, blossom with devotion whilst devotees themselves grow in true friendship and admiration for each other. All dialogue is mutually relished, whether they speak of, or hear about His virtues, His mercy, His incarnations or His phenomenal extraordinary divine pastimes. From speaking or hearing about His pastimes, a wonderful feeling of indescribable happiness arises, and the devotees become completely satisfied within. The *gopis* say the same in the *Srimad Bhagwatam* (10.31.9):

> Stories about You are the nectar of immortality for those dying in separation from You. Described by the great poets and dispelling sinfulness at their appearance, they are famous throughout the world; full of light and holiness, they grant the greatest auspiciousness to all who hear. Indeed, those who share Your stories with others are the greatest givers.

Therefore, a deep love for hearing the Lord's stories is declared as a mark of real devotion and one is also able to realise Him through this form of devotion.

Sutra 18

|| *ātmaratyavirodheneti śāṇḍilyaḥ* ||

Sage Shandilya believes that devotion for the Lord results from renouncing all barriers which deviate one from taking pleasure in Him.

The Sanskrit version of this aphorism begins with *ātmarati*,[23] which literally means pleasure in the self. The mind is composed in such a way that it constantly seeks after sense-pleasure. It is the nature of man to take a profound interest in himself, and this is known as selfishness. A person who is selfish pursues pleasure, but instead, he experiences despair due to the temporary nature of worldly objects, and therefore, the enjoyment is short-lived.

Due to this strong inclination towards material pleasure, the devotee should take extra care not to be diverted away from his devotional practice by engaging in sense-pleasure. These desires should not hinder one from taking delight in the Self, where the Self denotes realisation of the Lord in one's heart. According to Shandilya, devotion is to take the devotee's soul into that state of consciousness where he becomes one with the Supreme Being.

---

[23] The meaning of the word *ātmarati* here is described in a general context. The word self with a lower case s means that one does not have realisation of the Lord. Usually, one who is *ātmarati* is selfish unless one takes pleasure in the Lord who is realised is in one's heart and in this case the self becomes Self.

Sutra 19

|| *nāradastu tadarpitākhilācāratā tadvismaraṇe paramavyākulateti* ||

However, Narad feels that devotion consists of offering all activities to the Lord and the feeling of extreme distress by the devotee if He is forgotten.

Unlike the previous three aphorisms, here Sage Narad is giving his personal view on devotion, which he feels is the most complete, compared to those stated by others. He is not contradicting the opinions of Vyasdev, Garg and Shandilya. Vyasdev states that worship of the Lord is performed using one's body (*puja*). Garg states that hearing the pastimes of the Lord is devotion unto Him, and Shandilya states that an aspirant who realises the Lord in his heart worships Him with his mind. In his definition, Sage Narad declares that all three forms of worship (worship performed by the body, speech and mind) are necessary in devotion.

Devotion is the eternal unbreakable relationship between the Lord and the soul as His eternal servant. Just as a cluster of clouds does not know the powerful influence of the wind, similarly, a person engaged in material consciousness does not know the strength of time, which carries him. The person feels he controls everything when in fact it is time that controls him. For the sake of worldly happiness, the materialist works like a machine and the Lord destroys whatever he produces in time. For this reason, a person who is not a devotee grieves for his losses.

The misguided materialist does not know that his body is impermanent and the attractions of home, land and wealth, which have a relationship with the body alone, are also temporary. Out of ignorance, he thinks that everything is permanent and performs actions for himself and his family, and for society. Lord Krishn guides Arjun to renounce all actions executed for himself, and instead, dedicate all of his actions as *yagya* (a ritual of offering made to the Lord). In each action one performs, one should always try to take direction from the Lord. Surrendering both desire and attachment, and thereby becoming free from ego conceptions of I-ness or my-ness and any ideas of ownership, one should cheerfully perform all actions for the satisfaction of the Lord. For such souls, Narad is simplifying the definition of devotion. The *Bhaktirasamrtasindhu* (1.2.200), quoting the *Pancaratra*, mentions, "O Sage! If one desires devotion, one should perform actions, both worldly and spiritual, as a loving offering to the Lord."

Hence the first point of this aphorism states that all activities are to be directed towards the Lord throughout one's life. The second point raised herein is the feeling of extreme distress if the devotee forgets the Lord. This is the essence of devotion. Devotion is not exclusively happiness or joy; devotion never gives joy alone. The path will give intense pain at times. The *gopis* are a great example of this. In devotion, the sorrow felt by the *gopis* is defined as the burden of pain in the heart due to mental and physical separation from their Beloved, Lord Krishn. In the *Srimad Bhagwatam* (10.19.16), "When the *gopis* saw Krishn returning home, they were immersed in bliss, since for them, a moment without Him was like a hundred ages."

A single moment's separation from Lord Krishn felt like millions of years for the *gopis*. Chaitanya Mahaprabhu says in the *Sikshastakam*, "A blink of the eye is like millions of lifetimes for me and my eyes pour like monsoon clouds. The whole Universe is void to me, in estrangement from Krishn."

Extreme anguish is another sign of devotion, which is not unnatural. When a devotee practices one-pointed devotion for the Lord and he is in communion with Him, the devotee feels content, but the moment the devotee forgets the Lord, even for a second, it causes extreme pain in him. The life of a devotee is a mixture of happiness and sadness of the most extraordinary intensity. When one has attained this state of complete loving absorption for the Lord, formal religious practices are no longer required.

Sutra 20

|| *astyevamevam* ||

Devotion is correctly described in this way alone.

In the previous aphorisms, Narad showed the different understandings of Vyasdev, Garg and Shandilya, but here, Narad concludes that his definition is the most suitable, and Narad defines the highest form of devotion. In aphorism 19, Narad said that, "Devotion consists of offering all activities to the Lord and the feeling of extreme distress by the devotee if He is forgotten." And in this aphorism, Narad solidifies his definition by stating, "Devotion is correctly described in this way alone." This is not based on a mere theory or statement; it comes from his personal experience. In the next aphorism, Narad gives an example to prove this declaration.

Sutra 21

|| *yathā vrajagopikānām* ||

A great example of the exact nature of this devotion is that of the *gopis*, the cowherd women of Vraj.

All devotees consider the *gopis* of Vraj the perfect role models of devotion, and Sage Narad uses them as the finest exemplars of the devotion that he has characterised. In the *Srimad Bhagwatam* (10.44.15), the women of Mathura[24] state:

> The *gopis* are most fortunate, for their minds dwell on Krishn constantly. With love in their hearts and trembling voices, they sing about Him as they milk their cows, thresh grain, churn butter, care for the children of their households, clean and do their other chores. All good and auspicious things come to them due to their glorious state of mind.

The great love of the *gopis* can be understood by the symptoms they showed when they heard the sound of Krishn's flute:

> The sound of Krishn's flute provoked the *gopis'* love for Him and the desire to be with Him. He had already brought their hearts under His sway and now He stole all fear, hesitation, self-control and social obligations from their minds. As soon as they heard the flute, they began to act very strangely. The *gopis*, who had performed worship to get Krishn as their Husband, started sneaking out of home without telling the other *gopis*. They ran so fast that the earrings swayed in their ears. Others had been milking cows, but the moment they heard the sound of the flute they stopped and ran towards the sound. Some left milk on the stove, and some left food cooking there. Some had been dressing themselves, serving food to their families, feeding milk to children, or serving their husbands, but they dropped everything to go and meet Krishn. Other *gopis* were eating dinner, while some were bathing, getting dressed or touching up their eyeliner, but they all dropped everything, even the ones whose makeup and ornamentation was only half done. Their husbands, brothers and other relatives tried to stop them and place obstacles in the path of their blessed love-journey, but Krishn had captivated their hearts and minds.

---

[24] Mathura is a city in Uttar Pradesh (India) and it was Lord Krishn's maternal home.

> They were so enthralled that nobody was able to stop them. How could they succeed, for the Enchanter of the Universe, Krishn, had kidnapped their minds, hearts and souls. Entranced by the song of the flute, they refused to go home again. But some of the *gopis* could not escape their houses. They remained there with their eyes closed, meditating upon Him with great love and absorption. (*Srimad Bhagwatam* 10.29.4-9)

In the *Srimad Bhagwatam* (10.47.61), Uddhav, a great devotee of the Lord, said, "Blessed are the *gopis* of Vraj! They have renounced their families, which is very difficult to do, and have traded the path of piety for refuge at Krishn's feet. I wish to become a blade of grass, a vine or a plant in Vrindavan, so that I may receive the dust of their lotus feet upon my head eternally."

Lord Krishn said to the *gopis*, "My dear *gopis*! I shall never be able to repay you for all that you have done for Me, even if I try for a lifetime of the gods. You have truly loved Me, breaking the chains of household life, which is very difficult to do. May your own wonderful actions be your reward." (*Srimad Bhagwatam* 10.32.22)

Krishn continuously praises the *gopis*, "Names and forms merge in the trances of meditating sages, just as great rivers merge into the sea. In the same way, the *gopis* also lost all awareness of their bodies, the world, their families and the future in their constant thoughts of Me." (*Srimad Bhagwatam* 11.12.12)

The example of the sages in meditation is mentioned here only to illustrate concentration on a single object. The *gopis* simply loved Krishn and could not think of anything else. They cast off all obstacles that obstructed their concentration whilst they were remembering Krishn, cursing even their own eyelids for blinking and thus removing Krishn from their sight for a split second. From the *Srimad Bhagwatam* (10.30.43):

> The hearts of the *gopis* had become saturated with Krishn. They constantly thought of only Him and spoke about Him. Everything they did was for Him. Krishn had permeated their every pore; their souls were full of Him. They only meditated on His magnificent deeds and sang His glories. They were so absorbed in Him that they did not even remember their own bodies. How could they possibly think of home?

If a person has a duty to perform but due to some difficulty he cannot complete it, he simply gives up. But when Krishn disappeared from the *Raas Mandal*,[25] the *gopis* were searching for Krishn everywhere, asking the vines, the trees and the deer if they had seen Him; still they could not find Him anywhere. Yet the *gopis* did not return to their homes. Even though they could not find Krishn, their homes and families had been completely forgotten. The *gopis* became completely absorbed in the remembrance of Krishn only; it was as if they were possessed. Taking on the Lord's identity, they began imitating His activities and saying to one another, "How graceful is my gait? How beautifully do I play the flute?" Intoxicated in His love, they were not aware of what they were doing. They became so absorbed in the Lord that their natures changed and they forgot everything. As the *gopis* searched for Krishn, they only remembered His virtues and His pastimes with them, whereas usually people think mostly of their material comforts and are easily capable of forgetting devotion for the Lord.

In the *Vidagdh Madhav*, the mother of Sage Sandipani, Purnamasi, speaks to Nandimukhi:

> O Nandi! Radha's heart churns with great waves of intense love; Her actions are indescribable. All this is happening by the influence of the great Hero of romantic love. How amazing! Sages meditate on Him after traversing beyond the material worldly qualities, and with great effort they establish Him in their hearts. But this young Lady is trying desperately to stop thinking about that same Krishn so that She can concentrate on Her household chores. How strange that She is trying to get Him out of Her heart - the same Person whom the sages try desperately to capture in their hearts by intense spiritual practice and austerity!

Here, Radha, the Queen of the *gopis,* is so saturated with the love of the Lord that She is completely intoxicated with thoughts of Him and She is unable to function in Her household. Fearing that Her family will chastise Her, Radha desperately tries to remedy this, only to fail in Her endeavour, making Her more anxious. To experience a mere drop of this love, the sages had to perform austeries for thousands of years. This is the splendour of the Lord's sacred love, and its attainment is the supreme goal of the soul. The love of the *gopis* is unique because it is constant, undiluted and unconditional. For devotees, the *gopis* of Vraj are the height, the very essence of pure love. Hence, Sage Narad has used them as the topmost example.

---

[25] The *Raas Mandal* was a place where the Divine Dance was performed between Lord Krishn, Radha and the rest of the *gopis*.

Sutra 22

|| *tatrāpi na māhātmyajñānavismṛtyapavādaḥ* ||

Even in the case of the *gopis*, one cannot criticize that they were not aware of the Lord's divine personality.

The *gopis* were condemned and accused of having sexual desires for Krishn, and they were also blamed for not being conscious of His divine personality. The women of Vraj are criticized by those who are not able to view this love as anything other than sexual lust. Even King Parikshit, who listened to a discourse on the *Srimad Bhagwatam* from Sage Shukdev, could not understand the depth of their love and questioned the orator: "Oh sage! The *gopis* only thought of Krishn as their Lover, not understanding that He is the Ultimate Reality. So how could these girls, deluded by the threefold qualities of material existence, become free?" (*Srimad Bhagwatam* 10.29.12)

Sage Shukdev tried to clear King Parikshit's misunderstanding about the *gopis* by pointing out that what really mattered was the love the *gopis* felt for Lord Krishn and their constant meditation upon Him. Yet Parikshit was not able to understand this and raised his doubt again. This time, Shukdev said that divine beings should not be judged by human standards. Lord Krishn states in the *Srimad Bhagwatam* (10.22.26), "For those who have offered their hearts and souls to Me, their desires do not lead to further desire, just as grains dried under the sun and then cooked cannot germinate."

The *gopis* indeed were attracted to Krishn in the mood of romantic love, but this love should not be compared to material lust. Their desire became the highest form of love for the Lord. The *Srimad Bhagwatam* (10.31.4) clears this doubt: "You are not only the Son of Yashoda, but the indwelling Witness in the hearts of all beings. You are the One who Brahma prayed for, and now You have come in the dynasty of the Yadus[26] to save the world." Those who do not understand the unconditional love of the *gopis* for the Lord will misconstrue texts describing the *Raas Mandal* as erotic and impure. From the following *Srimad Bhagwatam* verse (10.31.19), one can even misinterpret the virtuous mood of the *gopis* as lusty:

---

[26] The Yadus are descendents of King Yadu.

> Oh Beloved! Your lotus feet are so tender and our breasts are hard. Thus, we place Your feet on our breasts extremely gently, fearing we may hurt them. You are life itself for us! The mere thought of Your soft lotus feet walking bare on the path at night, vulnerable to injury by sharp stones, fills us with constant anxiety.

The amorous desire of the *gopis* in this quote is pure unconditional love. It is an expression of love because the *gopis* were only concerned with pleasing the Lord, disregarding even their own pleasure:

> One may propose that amorous love for the Lord is sinful, assuming that scripture will support such an assumption. However, nowhere in the scripture is amorous love for Him prohibited. There is no inherent problem with amorous desire for the Lord, and there is certainly no fault when amorous desire is combined with the feeling of being married to Him. (*Bhakti Sandarbh,* section 320)

Sage Shukdev glorifies this feeling in the *Srimad Bhagwatam* (10.90.27), "Who can imagine what kind of austerities these women must have done; these women who lovingly served the *Guru* of the entire Universe as their Husband, by massaging His feet, and so forth."

In the scriptures, one finds that even the great sages develop such feelings: "The sons of the fire god, who were great souls, performed austerities in order to attain female bodies and attained Krishn, the birthless and omnipotent One, as their Husband." (*Kurm Puran*)

Amorous desire for the Lord, which leads one to consider Him as one's Lover, is also not sinful. The *gopis* themselves have addressed this point with the following words: "Oh Beloved! You told us it is a woman's duty to serve her husband, children and family. That's true. So let us fulfil that duty by serving You, since You are the most dearly Beloved, the most intimate Relation and the very Self of all beings." (*Srimad Bhagwatam* 10.29.32)

Sage Shukdev also confirms the same in the *Srimad Bhagwatam* (10.33.36): "He dwells in the souls of the *gopis* and their husbands and within all beings. He is the indwelling Witness and the true Husband of all, and He has manifested His divine body in this world to enact His divine play." Even Lord Krishn confirmed the purity of the *gopis*' amorous love, "Your love is completely pure and without fault." (*Srimad Bhagwatam* 10.32.22)

Like the *gopis*, others have also attained this type of relation with the Lord, as mentioned in the *Uttar kand* of the *Padma Puran*: "The great sages, meditating in the Dandak forest, saw Lord Ram (an incarnation of Lord Krishn) when He came to visit their hermitages. When they saw His enchanting form, they desired Him. Later, they attained female bodies and took birth in Gokul,[27] where they attained the eternal Lord Krishn as their Beloved."

Therefore, this amorous passion of a woman for her lover appears even in men, and because it is directed towards the Lord, it is not material passion encouraged by the material Cupid. Rather, it is completely spiritual because only the Lord, who is worshipped in the scriptures as the Father of Cupid, arouses it. People who are carried away with their own understanding (the lusty nature of the *Raas Mandal* and the activities which took place there) fail to realise that the *gopis* did not see the Lord as an ordinary man and they were never absent-minded about Lord Krishn's divine personality. Therefore, love directed towards the purest object of love, Lord Krishn, cannot be lust; it can only be sacred love.

[27] Gokul is a town near Vrindavan where Lord Krishn spent His early childhood.

Sutra 23

|| *tadvihīnaṁ jārāṇāmiva* ||

Love without the knowledge of His true nature is like an illicit affair.

In this aphorism, Sage Narad disagrees with the idea that the *gopis* were not aware of Lord Krishn's divinity. As soon as an ordinary man or woman sees an image of Radha and Krishn, he or she immediately thinks Their relationship is non-different from an earthly illicit affair, because on Earth, one perceives the highest form of love to be that which exists between a husband and wife, and therefore this inappropriate comparison is made. Narad states that if lack of spiritual awareness is present, then Radha and Krishn's union is perceived as some kind of earthly desire, just as men or women may have towards their lovers. This is by no means comparable to what Radha and the rest of the *gopis* felt for the Lord. Love that is based on the knowledge that the object of love is Krishn Himself has some special virtues of its own. Those who actually realised that Lord Krishn was the supreme object of their love, such as the *gopis*, experienced indescribable joy and the utmost privilege of enjoying this untainted divine bliss.

Sutra 24

|| *nāstyeva tasmiṁstatsukhasukhitvam* ||

In lust, there is a tendency for self-satisfaction, and no pleasure is derived by making the Beloved happy.

In love, there cannot be any trace of selfishness. But when one has desire, there is an expectation that the fulfillment of his desire will satisfy him. For example, if a man loves flowers, he will pluck and smell them, crush them, and throw them away. Or he will use them to decorate his house until they die, and thereafter, he will dispose of them. This is the nature of desire. In business transactions, companies target wealthy investors and claim they want to maximise the investors' profits, when in actual fact, the companies have the desire to increase their own profit margins. In the same way, in worldly love, the idea is to make oneself happy and not to make the object of love happy. Any earthly love or relationship transforms into bitterness when there is some irritation in the relationship. If a man is emotional and in love and this love is not returned, his feelings will change into bitterness because a lustful lover loves his paramour only for his own pleasure (for the gratification of his own senses). He does not derive joy from the happiness of his beloved. On the contrary, pure love seeks the happiness of the beloved only, without consideration for personal satisfaction, and the lover delights in the joy of serving his beloved in this way.

There are various moods in love. One can adore the Lord as one's Master and become His servant. This is a very simple mood. Or if one can rise higher still, one can think of the Lord as one's Friend. When one thinks of the Lord as his Friend, both are almost on the same level as each other. If a devotee can advance further, then he can love the Lord as his Child and can become His parent. Finally, one can reach the highest form of love, *Madhurya Ras*, a profound love between two lovers; one which merges the two hearts into one. The *gopis* did not desire any physical contact with Lord Krishn. Their profound and chaste love always searched for an opportunity to serve Krishn, solely for His pleasure. Their body, mind, intellect, physical charm, youth, wealth and life itself was offered to Him for His happiness. The *Chaitanya Charitamrit* (1.4.165-169) describes this love:

> The desire to please oneself is called lust but the desire to give Krishn pleasure is [sacred] love. A person experiencing lust pursues his own happiness, but in love, the devotee makes Krishn's pleasure the only goal. Thus, love is exceedingly powerful. The *gopis* did not care for society's expectations, the codes of conduct mentioned in the scriptures or their own bodily needs. They cast aside shyness, hesitation, physical comforts and their own personal happiness, and they embraced abuse from their families, all for Krishn's sake. The *gopis* do things for Krishn just for the sake of making Him happy. Their love is powerful and steadfast; it is completely pure, like a white cloth without a single spot. Thus, it can be understood that there is a great difference between lust and love. Lust is darkness whilst love is pure light. The love of the *gopis* does not have the slightest scent of lust. They carry on relationships with Krishn just so they can get a chance to make Him happy.

A devotee who experiences pure love feels the need to selflessly serve his Beloved. Impure or desirous love cannot enjoy the real happiness of serving because the nature of this love seeks self-satisfaction. Understanding this difference is the essence of Sage Narad's discourse in this aphorism.

4

The Excellence of Devotion

Sutra 25

|| *sā tu karmajñānayogebhyo'pyadhikatarā* ||

The path of devotion is superior to the path of action (*karm yog*), the path of knowledge (*gyan yog*) and the path of disciplined contemplation (*raj yog*).

There are four paths that lead the aspirant to the Lord: the paths of devotion, knowledge, action and disciplined contemplation. In this aphorism, Sage Narad tries to establish devotion as the highest path to attain Him. "A devotee is greater than one who relies on penance, intellect or purposeful action. Become a devotee. And the greatest of all devotees is one who worships Me with firm faith." (*Bhagwad Gita* 6.46-47)

"Neither *yog*,[28] *Sankhya*,[29] performance of social duties, scriptural study nor renunciation can captivate Me as mature devotion can." (*Srimad Bhagwatam* 11.14.20)

Many spiritual masters place greater importance on the paths of action, knowledge or disciplined contemplation, yet in the scriptures there are numerous examples which confirm the superiority of devotion.

1. The path of action: The *Bhakti Sandarbh* (section 99) reveals the uncertainty and misery involved in attaining the fruits of this path. But in the case of devotion, success is assured and the devotee experiences happiness even in the initial stage of devotional practice. In a conversation with Soot Maharaj, Sage Shaunak says, "We have been performing fire offerings unto the Lord for so long that our bodies have turned dark from the smoke. Still, success is not

---

[28] *Yog* here is the path of *raj yog*.

[29] *Sankhya* is one of the six orthodox schools of Hindu philosophy, which does not believe in the existence of a God.

assured. But you are giving us great joy by blessing us with the intoxicating and sweetest honey from the lotus feet of Lord Krishn." (*Srimad Bhagwatam* 1.18.12)

In the case of a fire offering (*yagya*), there is no assurance of success because there are many possibilities of making mistakes whilst performing the ritual; therefore success is in doubt. In the abovementioned *Srimad Bhagwatam* verse, one should understand that the uncertainty and hardship pointed out, specifically in relation to the fire offering, actually applies to all other forms of action, where action means performing tasks to please the Lord so that He will fulfil personal desires. Also in the *Brahmvaivart Puran*, Lord Vishnu said to Shiv (the lord of ignorance and a *Vaishnav*), "People certainly attain Me if they want Me. In *Kaliyug*,[30] it is futile to take refuge of social duty (thinking one can attain Me thereby). The lives of such people are wasted in *Kali,* but not so with those who take refuge in Me."

This can be understood by a story from the *Kartik Mahatmya* of the *Padma Puran*. "Once there was a *Brahmin*[31] named Vishnu Das, who lived in the kingdom of Chola.[32] He always offered pure and loving worship to the Lord. The king of Chola had a competition with Vishnu Das to see who could attain the Lord first. He prepared many sacrificial offerings and performed many ceremonies for the Lord, yet the king could not attain Him. Thereafter, he gave up on sacrifices and asked his priest Mudgal to advise him. The king said, 'I have made so many offerings, given charity, and done so many other things to compete with this *Brahmin,* but he has already attained a form like that of Vishnu[33] and is now being taken away to Vishnu's abode, *Vaikunth*!' Speaking thus, the king stood in front of the sacrificial fire and spoke the following words three times, 'Please grant me unwavering devotion to Vishnu (Krishn) in body, mind and speech.' Speaking thus with great humility and taking shelter of exclusive devotion to the Lord, he offered himself unto the sacrificial fire and gave his life up. Upon doing so, he immediately attained devotion."

---

[30] *Kaliyug* is the name of the present age in Hinduism, also known as the age of demise. It is the last of the four great ages (*Satyug, Dwapar Yug, Treta Yug and Kaliyug*).

[31] A *Brahmin* is a priest of the highest caste.

[32] The Chola Empire was one of the longest ruling dynasties (primarily in southern India).

[33] Here, Vishnu is an incarnation of Lord Krishn and not the devotee Vishnu Das.

In the *Bhaktirasamrtasindhu* (1.2.246-247), Lord Krishn says, "The wise devotees do not accept social duty as a devotional practice. One should take refuge of such duties only until one has developed indifference towards them or until faith arises for sharing stories about Me." Therefore, one can conclude that Lord Krishn is not pleased merely by sacrifices and acts of charity. Devotion alone is the cause of His pleasure.

2. The path of knowledge: This philosophy states that knowledge need not be taught because it is already present within. Knowledge is merely covered by ignorance, in other words, one is unaware that this Universe and everything that it contains is just an illusion. This false impression can be removed by the practice of self-realisation, where the self or the soul merges with the Supreme Soul or *Brahman*[34] by meditation. Therefore, spiritual masters of the path of knowledge support their philosophy by quoting the *Bhagwad Gita* (5.15), where Lord Krishn says, "Knowledge is covered by ignorance that bewilders the living beings." However, when Lord Krishn says that ignorance covers knowledge, He actually means that a person loses the ability to make proper decisions because he does not have knowledge of himself or external knowledge and thus, he is in a state of confusion. In this instance, knowledge of the self needs to be taught, and this knowledge is gained by the practice of devotion, which opposes the argument made by the followers of the path of knowledge (*gyanis*).

In reality, when one starts to analyse the understanding of the *gyanis*, many questions arise. If the Self (or the soul realised in *Brahman*) is full of knowledge, then why does one question who one is and what one's true purpose is? Just as darkness can never cover light, ignorance can never hide knowledge. Darkness is nothing but an absence of light, and ignorance is nothing but an absence of knowledge. To cover something, the covering agent must have positive existence, and darkness and ignorance are not positive entities.

Moreover, in the *Bhagwad Gita* (4.39), Lord Krishn says that a man of faith who attains knowledge (*gyan*) becomes peaceful. If this knowledge was already within man, there would be no need to attain it in the first place. In the *Bhagwad Gita* (7.2), Lord Krishn declares to Arjun, "I will now impart this knowledge unto you." Again, why would the Lord waste His time if Arjun's soul already possessed this

---

[34] *Brahman* is the Lord without a form, also known as the Absolute.

knowledge? The Lord removes ignorance by giving Arjun knowledge of his soul.

Lord Krishn speaks of knowledge and ignorance as part of His illusionary energy (*maya*): "O Uddhav, both knowledge and ignorance, which cause liberation and bondage to the human beings, are two primordial energies created by My *maya*." (*Srimad Bhagwatam* 11.11.3)

Scriptures often state that knowledge gives liberation. Here knowledge is to be interpreted as devotional knowledge, because, although one can acquire objective knowledge about Him by reading the scriptures, the Lord can only be attained by the practice of devotion: "After knowing Him, one should practice devotion." (*Brihadaranyak Upanishad*)

According to the *gyani*s, the Universe is a matrix of illusion or a dream. In simple terms, a fruit consists of seeds, shell and pulp. If one rejects one of the fruit's constituents, then what parts of the fruit determine its real nature? If one wants to know the weight of a fruit, one must weigh the seeds, shell, pulp and all the other components that make up the fruit. The *gyani* effectively rejects the existence of all elements of creation and only accepts the Creator by insisting that everything except *Brahman* is a dream. But to define the Universe as a dream is not accurate. In fact, it is a reality which is temporary in its nature. For example, if creation is a dream and a person commits murder, he is not punished for it and no one else is affected by his actions. But in this world, when a person kills, he is punished for it and the death has an impact on those connected to the victim. One who follows the path of devotion does not deny any element of the world because one's Lord is the Creator and He exists in everything. Devotional scriptures use the dream analogy in a slightly different context. They use it to illustrate the temporary nature of this world.

> By drinking the nectar of Your story, the hearts of the devotees are purified. They attain enlightened understanding of You, achieve dispassion towards all material things and easily reach Your eternal abode. Others conquer their lower natures and attain You through meditation, but this is very difficult, whereas a devotee attains You simply and painlessly just by serving You with love. (*Srimad Bhagwatam* 3.5.45-46)

Therefore, the scriptures praise the superiority of the path of devotion above the path of knowledge.

3. The path of disciplined contemplation: *Yog* means to yoke or to join. In *raj yog* or *ashtang yog*, the word *ashtang* means the eight limbs, in other words the eight stages, where the physical practice of postures and breathing techniques are a small aspect of the overall path. The goal or the eighth limb is the union of the soul with the Lord. Traditionally, the sages and seers performed these physical exercises in order to prepare the body, heart, and mind for sense withdrawal, concentration, meditation and thereafter, union with the Lord. The mind and body are purified[35] by the performance of postures (*asans*), breath control (*pranayam*), cleansing techniques (*kriyas*) and meditation (*dhyan*). This path was traditionally practiced for the sole purpose of spiritual satisfaction. If this motivation is absent, it is not technically *raj yog*. Yet this path is still not superior to devotion and the reasons are explained by Lord Krishn to Muchukund:

> Oh King, a person who is not a practitioner of devotion tries in various ways to control his mind but cannot overcome the craving for sensory pleasures, even through breath control and other practices. Thus, his mind often reverts to focusing on that which attracts the senses. (*Srimad Bhagwatam* 10.51.61)

Therefore, to attain the Lord, the path of devotion (above all other practices and actions which do not serve Him directly) is superior.

---

[35] Initially, one practices the *yams* (the restraints) and *niyams* (the observances) before progressing onto the physical aspects of *asthang yog*.

Sutra 26

|| *phalarūpatvāt* ||

Devotion is the process to attain the goal and the goal itself; devotion is the means and the end.

tīrthāṭan sādhan samudāī, jog birāg gyān nipunāī
nānā karam dharam brat nānā, sañjam nem gyān bigyānā
bhūtadayā guru dvij sevakāī, vidyā vinay bibek baṛhāī
jahań lagi sādhan bed bakhānī, sab kar phal hari bhagati bhavānī

> "The *Veds* describe pilgrimage, spiritual practice, *yog*, renunciation, scholarship, social duty, religious observances, vows, self-control, compassion towards all living things, service of the *guru* and *Brahmins*, personal study and cultivation of wisdom. All this and more is discussed in the scriptures but devotion to Krishn is the result (goal) of all these efforts." (*Vrajwasi Poetry*)

According to the *gyani*, identity of the Self remains hidden if one identifies oneself with the five material barriers, three bodies and three states of consciousness,[36] which cover knowledge of the Self. By the process of meditation, real knowledge of one's true identity is uncovered, and thereafter, one merges with *Brahman*. When the *gyani* becomes *Brahman*, he has no object to meditate upon. The *raj yogi* practises the eight limbs, to rein his senses and his mind, in order to realise that he is the soul and not the body. Through his practice, the *raj yogi* realises that his true identity is characterised by blissfulness that comes with liberation from the worldly worries and suffering, and thereafter, he remains content in this realisation. The *karm yogi* perceives all the names and forms of the world as a manifestation of the Lord. Thus, he physically and selflessly serves everything in nature in order to realise *Brahman*. In such paths, the means to reach the goal and the goal itself are different. In the case of the path of devotion, from the very beginning, one knows that he practices love for the Lord to attain love for the Lord; therefore, devotion is the process to attain the goal and that devotion/love is the goal itself. Therefore, devotion is the means and the end.

---

[36] Five material barriers: earth, water, fire, air and space. Three bodies: physical, subtle and causal. Three states of consciousness: waking, dreaming and deep sleep.

Sutra 27

|| *Īśvarasyāpyabhimānadveṣitvād dainyapriyatvāc ca* ||

Because the Lord dislikes pride and loves humility.

In the 25th aphorism, Sage Narad establishes the superiority of devotion over the other paths. In the 26th aphorism, he explains that devotion itself is the only path, and one who follows this path sincerely will obtain the goal, which is devotion itself. This is not the case when one endeavours to follow the paths of knowledge, action and disciplined contemplation. Here, Narad introduces another argument by stating that devotion removes pride from the devotee and bestows humility unto him, which the Lord welcomes.

Typically, on the path of knowledge the follower thinks that he is supreme and that he is the Lord Himself. On the path of devotion, there are two individuals: the Lord and His devotee. If the devotee believes he is the Lord Himself then who shall worship whom? A follower of the path of action often feels pride when he performs good deeds and rituals, and he frequently enjoys the egoistical idea of being a pious and good devotee.

On the path of disciplined contemplation, the aspirant becomes proud of his austere discipline. He is able to show others how he has mastered his physical body by performing postures to impress them. At a certain point in his practice, the aspirant attains mystic powers (*siddhis*) and he is able to manipulate the forces of nature to perform great acts of wonder. In time, he starts to feel that he is the source behind the power. An aspirant may divert his attention away from his true goal (uniting his soul with the Lord through meditation), and instead, use his body and mind to demonstrate his capabilities before others. Therefore, humility in such paths is not completely pure.

In the *Mahabharat*[37] when the Pandavs (five brothers) gambled with the Kauravs (their cousins), they lost all of their assets, including their wife Draupadi (Draupadi was married to all five brothers). Dushaasan, who was on the side of the Kauravs, grabbed Draupadi and started to disrobe her in full view of her husbands and her

---

[37] The *Mahabharat* is one of the great Hindu epics and it chronicles the battle between the Pandavs and the Kauravs. The *Bhagwad Gita* is a section of this epic.

respected elders. She prayed to Lord Krishn for help and He arrived, taking the form of an endless piece of cloth, to save her.

After this incident Draupadi asked Krishn, "Why did You come so late to save me?"

Krishn replied, "When you called, 'Go,' from, 'Govind,'[38] I left My city Dwarka[39] to save you, and when you said, 'Vind,' I reached Hastinapur.[40] But I could not do anything because you held on to your cloth with the pride and attitude that only your hands could save you. The moment you let go of the cloth, I appeared to save you."

Egotism can appear in any form, even within devotees. For example, a devotee may compare himself with other devotees. He may feel that he serves more people or that he follows the code of conduct more appropriately than others. Therefore, the devotee harbours thoughts that are also a part of pride. Hence, Chaitanya Mahaprabhu instructs in the *Sikshastakam* (verse 3), "We should become humbler than a blade of grass and more tolerant than a tree. Free from pride, we should offer respect to others and we should sing the praises of Krishn unceasingly." A devotee never expects any honour from anyone, yet he honours all living entities at all times, knowing that his beloved Lord dwells in all of them. In the following *Srimad Bhagwatam* verse (11.2.41), the characteristics of a devotee are described: "He bows to the sky, air, fire, water, earth, stars, directions, trees, oceans and all beings, knowing all that exists is the Lord's own body."

When a devotee is overwhelmed with intense love for the Lord, he sees the manifestation of his dearest Lord wherever he turns and he bows to everyone with humility. Whilst defining humility, Sanatan Goswami states, "Humility is what makes a person feel himself to be lowly, though he may truly be the most advanced. The wise practitioner should act according to the example set by the great ones who have attained such humility. In thought, word and deed they should never act otherwise." (*Brhad Bhagwatamrit*)

When a devotee is truly humble, he is also mindful, which makes him feel accountable even if the slightest feeling of personal authority emerges from him. Sanatan Goswami speaks highly of humility and

---

[38] Govind is another name for Krishn.

[39] Dwarka was the dwelling place of Lord Krishn, where He ruled for several years.

[40] Hastinapur, the city where this gambling match was taking place, was one of the greatest kingdoms of ancient India, where all the incidents in the epic of *Mahabharat* took place.

states that there is little difference between humility and devotion. Each is a driving force for the other. In the *Chaitanya Bhagwat,* a great humble devotee named Haridas Thakur tolerated the beatings of Muslims in twenty-two market places. When the Muslims tried to beat him to death, Haridas Thakur prayed to the Lord for the welfare of those who had committed these crimes against him: "Oh Krishn! Have mercy on them! Be not offended to see them torturing me like this!"

The essence of humility in devotion is very eloquently captured by the following story. In Vraj, there was an educated person from Bengal who had a desire to live in Vrindavan and take initiation[41] from a genuine spiritual master. He was inclined towards one particular spiritual master and approached him many times for initiation. But after speaking with the aspirant, the spiritual master always refused and felt that this person was inwardly proud of the knowledge he possessed. One day the aspirant came and requested initiation from the spiritual master. The spiritual master asked him to bring a person or an object inferior to him within seven days, and if the aspirant succeeded, he would be initiated.

At first the aspirant thought, "There are so many people and objects who are inferior to me. In a matter of moments I will find someone I can bring back with me and present to my spiritual master." He started to search for faults in people but he could not find any worse than his own. Then he tried to find fault with the animals and birds, but again he was unsuccessful because animals and birds possess many qualities similar to and better than those of humans. He tried to find inferiority in the vines and the trees, but again he failed because trees are very tolerant. Even if a tree dries up and dies she will not ask for water from anyone. Rather, she will serve everyone with her fruits, wood, leaves and resin. The tree patiently tolerates the scorching sunrays in the summer, the pouring rain in the monsoon season and the freezing winters. There can be nothing or no one more tolerant than a tree.

The aspirant incessantly searched for six days, yet he did not find anyone inferior to him. On the seventh day, he went into the field to defecate, and in the middle of the act he thought, "This stool is inferior to me in all respects! I will let my spiritual master know," but he paused and reconsidered his original thought. "How can this be true? Before this substance came in contact with me it was an

---

[41] Initiation is a procedure where one officially takes shelter of a spiritual master and becomes his disciple, to learn how one can serve and please the Lord.

offering to the Lord. In a bid to stay alive, I wanted to feed my body, and only after this it became such a disgusting substance. Can there be anyone lower than a person who feeds himself blessed food and turns it into waste matter?"

The aspirant decided that this stool was even better than him. Then he saw a worm crawling into the stool. He was overjoyed, thinking he had finally found someone beneath him, but soon after, he realised, "I have turned the Lord's food into stool and I cannot make it pure anymore, but this worm will surely merge this stool with the earth. This worm is not lower than me." After bathing, the aspirant went to his spiritual master and said, "After seven days of searching, I conclude that there is no creature or substance lower than me in this world."

The spiritual master smiled and said, "You have brought yourself here after surrendering your pride and accepting a humble attitude. Now you are ready for initiation." By the mercy of the spiritual master, the aspirant became a humble devotee of Krishn.

Sometimes, people show humility to project that they are better than others. To become a sincere devotee, one should never show authority over any other living being at any time. One should always remain as serene as a blade of grass, which gracefully bows under all forms of pressure. Bracing raging storms, the blade still returns to its natural form. One should stive to become more patient than a tree, which tolerates the harshest conditions, yet stands tall and shelters all. Until the aspirant develops this humility in the mind and in the performance of every action, pride will reside in his heart. Therefore, Sage Narad states that to be a beloved of the Lord, one must be humble and free of pride, and this is cultivated through the practice of devotion.

Sutra 28

|| *tasyā jñānameva sādhanamityeke* ||

According to some spiritual masters, devotion can only be attained through knowledge.

Devotion is loving service to the Lord, but in order to create the right emotional mindset for service, knowledge is needed. Narad does not refer to mere intellectual knowledge of the Lord. "Realisation achieved through intellectual analysis is not beautiful without thoughts of Krishn. How then can the hard path of purposeful action be beautiful if not performed as an offering solely for the Lord's pleasure?" (*Srimad Bhagwatam* 1.5.12)

Herein, the knowledge to be attained for the purpose of devotion is not the same as the knowledge one obtains from following *gyan yog*. *Gyan yog* leads to self-realisation, whereas the knowledge to understand the path of devotion leads to the realisation of the Lord and how one can please Him only.

One who understands that the Lord is the purest object of love, that He possesses countless attributes, that He is a Divine Form, that there is no one superior to Him and knows that He is worthy of love can engage in a loving relationship with Him. Only with clear instructions can one reach the correct destination without being misdirected. To understand the path of devotion and avoid misconceptions, knowledge is necessary. Even Buddh[42] preached that right understanding is the first step in his eightfold noble path to reach Nirvana.

[42] Buddh is commonly known as Buddha in the West and he is an incarnation of Lord Krishn.

Sutra 29

|| *anyonyāśrayatvamityanye* ||

Some spiritual masters say that knowledge and devotion are dependent on each other.

In this aphorism, Sage Narad states that according to the views of some spiritual masters, knowledge is dependent on devotion and devotion is dependent on knowledge. But one can say that a non-devotee who excels in the study of the scriptures will not realise the Lord in the way that a devotee will.

Lord Krishn Himself says, "If a person studies scripture but does not think of the Lord, his effort is fruitless, like that of a man who keeps a cow whose milk has dried up." (*Srimad Bhagwatam* 11.11.18)

Only the aspirant's devotion will make the Lord reveal Himself, whether he is knowledgeable in the scriptures or not, and this devotion is nothing but the most profound love one has for Krishn. Many great devotees were uneducated, and yet they attained the Lord by making a place in their heart for Him. The mutual dependency of knowledge (where knowledge is realisation of the Lord) and devotion may also mean that without the Lord there would be no devotee, but without a devotee, the Lord cannot be realised. Devotion itself contains that knowledge which is required to attain Him. By devotional practices and the shelter of a spiritual master, this knowledge is revealed.

Sutra 30

|| *svayaṁphalarūpateti brahmakumārah̤* ||

According to the sons of Brahma (Sanak, Sanandan, Sanatan, and Sanat Kumar), devotion is its own fruit.

Narad establishes his point of view on devotion, using the opinions of his elder brothers, the four Kumars, who are also his spiritual masters.

In the *Srimad Bhagwatam* (11.20.31), Krishn states that devotion does not depend on knowledge: "Therefore, for a practitioner on the path of devotion who meditates upon Me constantly, neither intellectual analysis nor renunciation is necessary." In the *Bhakti Sandarbh* (section 176), it is written, "Furthermore, devotion can grant the results of all other paths as a mere side-effect." And as stated by Lord Krishn:

> All that can be attained by others through purposeful action, austerity, intellectual analysis, *yog* (disciplined contemplation), charity, detachment, pious duties, and so forth, can be attained easily by My devotee through the power of devotion, along with residence in the material heavens, liberation, or residence in My eternal abode. (*Srimad Bhagwatam* 11.20.32-33)

Therefore, Lord Krishn and Sage Narad reject the path of knowledge. Naturally, one may feel that the shelter of knowledge should be taken to develop faith in the Lord. In anticipation of this assumption, the Lord explains the results of following the path of devotion: "Devotion is attained by association with My devotees. One who has attained devotion worships Me and experiences My direct presence. Then, by following the instructions of the saints, after purifying his heart, he attains My eternal abode as revealed by them." (*Srimad Bhagwatam* 11.11.25)

The process of devotion can grant all perfections easily, without reliance on any other method. This is expressed in the *Srimad Bhagwatam* (2.3.10): "A wise person, whether he be full of material desire, devoid of material desire or desirous of liberation, should worship the Lord by the path of devotion." Because the only duty prescribed for mankind is devotion: "Chanting of Krishn's Holy Name and other such devotional practices are the ultimate duty of all souls." (*Srimad Bhagwatam* 6.3.22)

The *Brhan Naradiya Puran* states, "Just as water is called 'the life of all beings,' so too is devotion the life of all perfections." There is a celebrated story of an old village woman who had a deep desire to worship Lord Krishn. She went to a spiritual master and asked him to give her instructions. The spiritual master took a round stone and gave it to her and said, "Take this rock and care for it as your child." The old woman took it and started taking care of it like her own flesh and blood. Every day she used to bathe and dress him beautifully. She offered him nice food and made him sleep on her lap. The village people started mocking her. One day, in jest, a villager said to her, "Beware! A wolf has been coming to the village for the last few days and he eats young children. Keep your child safe."

The old woman believed the villager's words and sat down, guarding her door with a wooden stick to protect her infant. She had no understanding of whom the Lord was or His powers. Three days passed without sleep, yet she served the stone day and night, sheltering it from any dangers. In the midst of her tension, the old lady had lost her appetite. On the fourth night, Lord Krishn came to her.

Startled by the presence of an unknown man, she heatedly demanded, "Who are you?"

"Mother, I am your Child, the One who you worship daily," Krishn replied.

She said, "I do not believe you."

Krishn said, "If you do not believe Me, then bring your infant with you. I will take you to My abode."

The old lady asked, "Can you assure me that there are no wolves in Your abode?"

Krishn spoke, "There are no lions or wolves, no flies or mosquitoes."

The old woman was delighted by the assurance that her son would live happily in Krishn's abode. She agreed, and Krishn gave the old woman His eternal shelter. This tale emphasizes that Lord Krishn can be attained by faith and not by knowledge. Thus, Sage Narad confirms that one reaches devotion through the practice of devotion only.

Sutra 31-32

|| *rājagṛhabhojanādiṣu tathaiva dṛṣṭatvāt* ||

|| *na tena rājaparitoṣaḥ kṣucchāntirvā* ||

For it is seen in the case of a regal palace and a meal, mere knowledge does not win the favour of the king, nor is one's hunger appeased by the sight of food.

Here, Sage Narad emphasises that one cannot build a personal relationship with the king just by knowing information about him, such as where he lives, the nature of his character, what he thinks of his well-wishers, and so forth. Similarly, just knowing who the Lord is gives Him no satisfaction unless one has cultivated feelings of love for Him.

A man went to the palace of a king. At the main gate, the guard stopped him and asked, "Who are you and who do you want to meet?"

"I want to meet the king," the man replied after introducing himself.

The guard asked, "Do you know the king?"

"Yes, I do," the man replied.

The guard asked, "The whole city knows him but does the king know you?"

"No, he does not know me," the man replied.

Therefore, the gatekeeper did not allow the man to pass. The king is not pleased when someone only knows who he is. Equally, mere knowledge of the Lord does not please Him, nor does it make one a devotee. If one wants to please the Lord, one must devote himself and serve Him solely for His pleasure. Furthermore, Narad states that if one is hungry, one cannot appease one's hunger by looking at a plate of food. One has to actually eat food to satisfy one's appetite.

Devotion is not dependent on knowledge. Knowledge cannot generate devotion; devotion can appear spontaneously, from the fruits of one's devotion in a previous life, by the mercy of a spiritual master, or by the mercy of the Lord. Knowledge can help to steer devotion in the right direction, but it is still secondary to the direct practice of devotion. The *Bhakti Sandarbh* (section 202) mentions, “Once one has understood the Lord intellectually by pondering scripture, one should then acquire realisation of who He truly is by serving Him.” Thus, Sage Narad stresses that knowledge of the Lord which does not increase one's love for Him only serves to please one’s ego.

Sutra 33

|| *tasmātsaiva grāhyā mumukṣubhiḥ* ||

Therefore, devotion alone is to be accepted by those who desire to cut all material bondages.

Whilst translating this aphorism, many spiritual teachers have stated, "Therefore, devotion alone is accepted by those who are desirous of liberation," which is contradictory because a devotee never yearns for liberation. His actions are not motivated by desire for personal happiness. He only seeks to give pleasure to his Lord.

A devotee's desire to love the Lord is reflected in the way he serves Him. In his commentary on the *Srimad Bhagwatam* (10.87.21), Shridhar Swami wrote, "Even souls liberated from the cycle of rebirth choose to be born again amongst men in order to worship Him."

Material bondages such as relationships, wealth, fame, and so forth, often become obstacles in devotional life and can prevent the aspirant from serving the Lord. Those who want to overcome these spiritual obstacles should take shelter of the path of devotion. "O Lord of the Universe! I do not want wealth, followers, fame, beautiful women or poetry. I only desire motiveless devotion for You birth after birth." (*Sikshastakam*, verse 4)

The *Chaitanya Charitamrit* states, "Sacred love is attained when desires for enjoyment, liberation and mystic perfections no longer exist in the heart." The mind of a devotee desires nothing but a deep longing to love and render service to his Lord. When he overcomes his attachments to worldly desires, the devotee can focus wholeheartedly on the devotional path and serve Lord Krishn. The *Narad Pancaratra* states, "Devotion means to serve the Lord of the Senses with the senses. Surrendering thus, one is purified and becomes free from selfish motivations." In the *Bhaktirasamrtasindhu* (1.1.11), Roop Goswami writes, "The highest kind of devotion is one in which the devotee constantly offers loving worship, care and service to Lord Krishn in a way which is pleasing to Him, free from any ulterior motive and not shrouded by reliance on intellectual knowledge (*gyan*) or purposeful action (*karm*)." He continues by asking, "How can devotional joy appear in a heart where the witchlike desires for material enjoyment and liberation dwell?" (*Bhaktirasamrtasindhu* 1.2.22)

When one has such desires, he tries to fulfil his own needs instead of pleasing the Lord, which is not pure devotion. When Lord Narsingh (an incarnation of Krishn) offered His devotee Prahlad a boon, Prahlad said:

> O Lord! O *Guru* of the entire Universe! I am terrified of attachment to material desires, and I took shelter of You desiring to renounce them. By nature, my heart is sullied by such desires, so please do not tempt me by offering material benedictions. Are You offering me such things, which would cause my heart's bondage to the material world, just so You could make my reaction an example for others? Otherwise, O Merciful One! How could You possibly offer to engage me in such unwanted and fruitless things? Those who serve You with the desire to get worldly things from You are not servants but businessmen. (*Srimad Bhagwatam*)

The merciful Lord never offers such things that create a knot in the heart binding a devotee to the material world. In the *Brhad Bhagwatamrit* (1.7.135), Narad Muni asks Krishn to fulfil a boon, "O Krishn! You are the personification of bliss! I pray that no one can ever be satisfied with their love and devotion for You but ever crave for more and more."

To which Krishn replies, "O Narad! What kind of boon is that? Everyone knows that mercy, love and devotion are infinite and inexhaustible."

Those who ask for material boons in exchange for their devotion are self-centred merchants. By offering money, flowers and sweets to the Lord, they try to obtain opulence or worldly happiness from Him. Lord Krishn states in the *Chaitanya Charitamrit*, "One who worships Me just to get material benefit is a great fool! He trades nectar for poison. But I am not a fool. Why should I give this fool worldly pleasures? Instead I will make him forget all about them by giving him the nectar of My lotus feet."

Therefore, devotion not only cuts the worldly bonds, it attracts the Lord to the aspirant, and once that connection is established, He Himself maintains the relationship.

Sutra 34

|| *tasyāḥ sādhanāni gāyantyācāryāḥ* ||

In hymns and songs, the spiritual teachers describe the means of attaining devotion.

"Those who are devoted with one-pointedness, who have surrendered themselves completely to the Lord, ask nothing from Him. They sink into the ocean of bliss as they sing of His amazing acts." (*Srimad Bhagwatam* 8.3.20)

On the path of devotion, the first step is to listen to the Lord's glories through His devotees: "One gets the chance to meet, speak with and serve great devotees if one lives in or visits holy places. By serving them, one attains faith and an interest for hearing about the Lord's acts. Upon hearing these stories, one develops a taste for them." (*Srimad Bhagwatam* 1.2.16)

Even if one wanders into a holy place for some other purpose, one automatically gets the opportunity to directly observe or speak with devotees who reside there, and these activities in themselves are also a type of devotional practice. By the influence of such practice, one develops faith in the devotees' character. The devotees naturally speak amongst themselves, glorifying the Lord, and a person who comes in contact with them develops a desire to hear. By hearing their conversations, he acquires a taste for them. Furthermore, when he hears from fully-realised devotees, the effect is immediate. The following verse confirms this:

> One gets the opportunity to hear the Lord's pastimes when one spends time with His devotees. These stories illustrate the process by which He may be attained; they give pleasure to the ears and the heart. Faith, attachment to the Lord and devotion to Him manifest quickly when one listens to these stories repeatedly. (*Srimad Bhagwatam* 3.25.24-25)

When that topmost stage of devotion manifests in a devotee, he experiences supreme celestial joy, which is mentioned in the scriptures and expressed by saints, seers and the spiritual teachers through songs and hymns. These masters attained the fruits of the practice for themselves and thus, by sharing the nectar of their realisations, they defined the path of devotion.

Sutra 35

|| *tat tu viṣayatyāgāt saṅgatyāgāc ca* ||

Devotion is attained through renunciation of objects of sense pleasure, as well as attachments to them.

The essence of the meaning of this aphorism can be illustrated by the story of a man who made the journey to visit a holy place. On his travels, he met a holy man who asked him to make an offering to please the Lord. The pilgrim thought about promising to give up the following food items: dairy products, vegetables or fruit. After some thought, he realised that he was unable to give up dairy products or any vegetable because he enjoyed eating these items and he felt that giving them up would cause him inconvenience, especially whilst eating out.

Although the pilgrim was fond of certain fruits, he decided to forfeit jackfruit, only because he disliked the fruit and did not personally consume it, nor was he likely to eat it in the future. He chose to forsake what he already had an aversion to. But this aphorism encourages the aspirant to forego and give up objects that can arouse his senses and disconnect him from the Lord.

When the heart is not clean, devotion cannot reside there. Generally, people either take shelter in what is advantageous for them or what gives them enjoyment. But the wise can understand the difference and always choose what is good for them. The foolish pursue what they like and what they do not have, whether it is good for them or bad. People have their own needs, yet it is possible to live if one does not acquire what one wants and likes: "One who understands the true meaning and goal of life should accept only as much wealth and goods as are needed for one's survival because excess and destitution both distract one from one's goal." (*Bhaktirasamrtasindhu* 1.2.108)

Those who cannot give up worldly pleasures argue that these desires are a necessary prelude to renunciation because only complete enjoyment of the desire will lead to satisfaction. In response, the *Mahabharat* states, "Indulgence never quenches desire but rather inflames it, just as oil poured on fire inflames it and does not put it out." King Bharat, who renounced his own family to advance in his spiritual life, became attached to an injured baby deer whilst he nursed it back to health. This diverted him from his spiritual progress: "In this way, his heart was agitated by a multitude of desires. Due to the reactions of his past life's actions, he lost his practice and was distracted from the Lord's worship. He became so attached to the fawn[43] that he forgot his own true nature." (*Srimad Bhagwatam* 5.8.26)

All the material objects of this Earth are not enough to satisfy a greedy man. Hence, Sage Narad advises that renunciation from attachment to such objects is just as compulsory as giving up the object itself. This point is highlighted in the following tale. After listening to the pastimes of the Lord from a realised soul, a wealthy man told his family that he was taking renunciation. He left his house, family, relatives and wealth and took the shelter of a forest. Whilst taking a stroll on a moonlit night, he noticed an object glistening on the ground. At first he thought it must be a pearl or an expensive gem. The man felt an impulse to grab it. When he touched it, he realised it was not a gem or pearl but human mucus shimmering in the moonlight. He felt awful, and he realised that if a drop of mucus created desire within him, he was not ready for complete renunciation. True renunciation is one where the renunciant has both physical and mental detachment from the object. To enjoy the taste of genuine devotion, dispassion for material objects is necessary.

When there is renunciation in the mind there is no incentive for enjoyment, and external renunciation (giving up the possession of an object) follows naturally. External renunciation is helpful in the early stages of devotion, whilst internal renunciation is essential at all times. Where complete renunciation is not possible, due to extenuating circumstances, one should at least practice mental renunciation and try to remain free from attachment to one's belongings. Thus, a mind free from the distractions of worldly objects and attachments to them becomes a receptacle for the love of the Lord. Therefore, Sage Narad states that the practice of both mental and physical renunciation is a necessity on the path of devotion.

---

[43] Fawn is a young deer.

Sutra 36

|| *avyāvṛttabhajanāt* ||

And through an uninterrupted offering of devotional practice to the Lord.

Here, Sage Narad reveals the method that nurtures the blossoming love, once an inclination to devote oneself to the Lord is awakened. He states that the practice should be uninterrupted. "Desire, anger and greed are three gateways to agony. They bring about one's destruction; one should give them up. Once freed from these three, one works for one's ultimate good and eventually attains the supreme goal." (*Bhagwad Gita* 16.21-22)

As soon as one enters the gateways of lust, greed and anger, one is not able to discriminate between what is favourable and what is not favourable for devotion. Therefore, the mind is apprehended and controlled by the senses.

Thus, Lord Krishn advises the avoidance of these passionate feelings, and to curb these emotions, Sage Narad strongly recommends uninterrupted practice of devotion. By doing so, the highest good and wellbeing of a human being is assured. "The greatest religion for the soul is one where there is devotion for Krishn that is unwavering and free from ulterior motives. Only this can completely satisfy the Lord." (*Srimad Bhagwatam* 1.2.6)

To clarify the exact nature of the practice, the *Bhaktirasamrtasindhu* (1.2.73) states, "According to the wise, one's devotional practice may either consist of a single type of practice or a combination of multiple types." There are 64 practices for a devotee, which are mentioned in the *Bhaktirasamrtasindhu*. By doing one or more of these practices uninterruptedly, one's devotion is strengthened. Uninterrupted means disciplined, stable, constant and punctual practice. In the *Bhagwad Gita* (8.14), Lord Krishn says, "He who remembers Me constantly and single-mindedly attains Me easily."

The *Madhurya Kadambani* describes a state experienced in the beginning of the devotional path. Often, devotees set goals for their personal practice: for example, the number of rounds to be chanted daily, the quantity of service to be rendered to devotees or simply not engaging in matters unrelated to the glorification of the Lord. Though such resolutions are made every day, the devotees are able to execute them some days and not others. Just as a relationship between two people requires a regular exchange and maintenance of love and affection, in the same way, the practice of service to the Lord should be an uninterrupted and unobstructed flow of devotion.

Sutra 37

|| *loke'pi bhagavadguṇaśravaṇakīrtanāt* ||

By listening to and singing His pastimes and glories, even while engaged in social life.

In the previous aphorism, uninterrupted practice in devotion is advised and in this aphorism, Sage Narad says that the service shall not be physical only. One who is preoccupied with the material world does not develop a mindset favourable for serving the Lord. In the present day, people rarely set aside time to serve Him daily. Sage Narad states that the main purpose of spiritual endeavour is to purify the mind in a simple way and in a manner where one can progress and attain devotion. According to Narad, this can be achieved by hearing the glories of the Lord. "Remember Me and do your duty. Centre your mind and heart on Me and you will come to Me without a doubt." (*Bhagwad Gita* 8.7)

One can cultivate this constant remembrance by hearing the glories of the Lord from elevated souls. "Lord Krishn enters the devotee's heart through his ears and enthrones Himself on the lotus of his love for Him. His presence washes away the impurities in His devotee's heart, just as monsoon rains overflow and cleanse pools of muddy water." (*Srimad Bhagwatam* 2.8.5)

One can hear the Lord's pastimes anywhere and at any time, but it is not enough to hear them from just any person. One must only hear from realised devotees. The speaker should be worthy of speaking on this divine subject, and the spiritual masters have made this point very clear. The *Brahmvaivart Puran* mentions two types of speakers:

1. *Saraag vakta*: One who gives his talks using music. This type of speaker is materialistic and greedy for money, celebrity status and power. He does not practice what he preaches and his words do not touch the heart. Listening to discourses given by such an ill-motivated speaker is harmful to the aspirant. In general, these speakers will not have much spiritual knowledge. They will persist in their inaccurate interpretation of the philosophy, having convinced themselves that the scriptures instruct such teachings. Vishwanath Chakravarti Thakur said, "The speaker should be one who has relished sacred love practically."

2. *Niraag vakta*: One who gives talks and does not use music as such, except when he sings the Holy Name. This type of speaker is one who is immersed in divine love. He presents the nectarine pastimes of the Lord, which infects the listener with a similar mood. He does not care for money, honour and glory.

Here, Sage Narad prescribes that aspirants should listen to the second type of speaker (the *niraag vakta*). According to the great devotee Binod Bihari Das Babaji from Barsana,[44] there are also two types of listeners. He states:

> In the countryside of Bengal, it is common to see people sitting quietly with a fishing rod near a river or pond. First the fisher scatters fish food in the water, then he attaches bait at the end of the hook, and finally, he sits in silence. The fish food has a very strong scent. Some fish are attracted, and they come rushing yet do not swallow the bait, and there are other fish who only nibble at the bait and move on. The last type of fish will immediately swallow the bait and get caught. This kind of fish struggles very hard to get away, yet what does the fisherman do? Instead of reeling it in, he loosens the line and allows the panicked fish to swim freely for some time. Once the fish becomes totally exhausted and gives up the fight, the fisherman reels it in easily.

Similarly, Lord Krishn has scattered His pastimes (like fish food) in this world. Some people come to hear them, but His glories have no impact on their hearts. They have some effect on others but do not leave a deep impression on them. These persons are like the fish who nibble the bait but do not swallow it. Yet there are those aspirants who, after hearing the pastimes of Lord Krishn from pure devotees, realise that devotional practice is the only goal of life, like the fish that swallow the bait. These aspirants are determined to obtain Lord Krishn. They start to develop a dislike for the material world, yet simultaneously, they do not get peace since they are unable to obtain Him. These aspirants still feel that they are the doer (the performer of action) and their devotion is imperfect. Thus, they continue to wander from one holy city to the next. Finally, in their misguided pursuits, these devotees exhaust themselves physically and emotionally. They fail to realise that happiness lies within and the spiritual journey itself is the real pilgrimage of discovery. The *Srimad Bhagwatam* (2.3.12) states:

---

[44] Barsana is a small town in Vraj.

> By listening to the stories of the Lord's holy acts, one attains that rare wisdom which calms the waves of life's ocean. The heart of the listener is delighted, his senses no longer cleave to worldly enjoyments and thus, he becomes a free soul. Who would not become addicted to such stories after relishing them once?

In addition to listening to the Lord's pastimes and His glories, Sage Narad asks the aspirant to sing His praises. Singing the Holy Name is a common practice of all religions. Krishn confirms the above statements to Arjun in the *Adi Puran*: "My dear Arjun! Those who sing and dance before Me, purchase Me. I become the slave of those who sing My Name and weep in front of Me, for I am Janardan (He who wipes away the tears of His dear ones). I do not belong to anyone else." The process of chanting the Holy Name is a reliable way to obtain sacred love:

> How should one chant so that sacred love arises? Listen Svarup and Ram Ray! Becoming humbler than a blade of grass and as tolerant as a tree, giving respect to all and not expecting any for oneself, one should chant the Holy Name always. Though acting in greatness, one should know oneself to be insignificant as grass. One should be as tolerant as a tree in two ways. Even when a tree is cut, she does not protest; though she dies of thirst, she begs not for water but instead she gives to all who come. She bears the heat and rain and offers everyone shelter. Similarly, a devotee should be great yet prideless. One should honour all life knowing that Lord Krishn dwells in all beings. If one chants the Holy Name in this way one shall receive sacred love for Lord Krishn. (*Chaitanya Charitamrit* 3.20.16-21)

The hearts and minds of non-devotees are stained and covered with desires for sensual enjoyments. Thus, Lord Krishn and His forms, His pastimes, and so forth, cannot be experienced by these persons.

> Glory to the collective singing of Sri Krishn's Holy Name, which cleanses the mirror of the heart and mind, which puts out the forest fire of worldliness, which casts moonlight upon the night-blooming lotus of auspiciousness, which is the life (husband) of the bride called wisdom, which causes high tide on the ocean of supernatural joy and which makes us relish immortal nectar as it bathes our whole soul. (*Sikshastakam*, verse 1)

The chanting of Lord Krishn's Holy Name cleanses the mirror of the heart. A clear mirror reflects a clear object. Similarly, the mirror of an aspirant's heart is purified through the process of singing the Name and dancing in ecstasy. As the level of purification increases, the experience of feelings from the Lord's pastimes, which an aspirant has felt before, become much sweeter. The body, organs, mind and intelligence are replenished when the body has an intake of food. Similarly, when one sings the Holy Name and dances to it, the whole self is nourished.

The *Bhakti Sandarbh* mentions four distinct types of singing:

1. Singing about the forms of the Lord
2. Singing about the virtues of the Lord
3. Singing the pastimes of the Lord
4. Singing the glories of the Lord

In this aphorism, Sage Narad offers a positive method to attain devotion; with a steady flow, let the mind and heart be constantly immersed in the Lord. Even if one remembers the Lord whilst eating, walking and sleeping, one can attain His devotion. One can listen to His pastimes and sing His praises even whilst engaging in social life.

In the 36th aphorism, Sage Narad elaborated on how one can develop devotion through the practice of uninterrupted service. Here, he takes his viewpoint a step further by saying that service or practice shall not be physical only. One can overcome the obstacle of being distracted with material issues whilst serving the Lord. Even in the present world, people have limited time to serve the Lord. Thus, in this aphorism, Sage Narad reminds the aspirant that the main purpose of spiritual effort is to purify the mind in a simple manner. By the method of hearing and singing, one can edge closer towards attaining devotion.

5

The Grace of Elevated Souls

Sutra 38

|| *mukhyatastu mahatkṛpayaiva bhagavatkṛpāleśād vā* ||

Primarily, through the grace of the great devotees, or through a little grace from the Lord.

In this aphorism, Sage Narad explains that the grace of great devotees is compulsory because without this mercy, one will find it hard to taste the nectar of Krishn's Holy Name or hear and sing it joyfully. The *Sikshastakam* (verse 2) states, "O Lord! You have mercifully given us Your many Names, full of Your power, without setting any rules on when and how they should be chanted. But I am greatly unfortunate for I still have no love for chanting them." The taste develops when one gets the association of pure devotees. All scriptures unanimously praise the importance of grace from devotees.

In the *Ramcharitmanas*, Jayant[45] went to test Lord Ram's power. At the time, Lord Ram was resting His head on the lap of His wife Sita, sleeping. In the form of a crow, Jayant descended and attacked Sita's face with his claws. Drops of blood fell from Her face onto Lord Ram's face, waking Him up. As a punishment, Ram recited a *mantra* to turn a small piece of straw into an arrow in order to kill Jayant. In fear, Jayant ran to take sanctuary of his father Indra, as well as Brahma and Shiv, but they all refused to give him shelter.

Witnessing Jayant's condition, Sage Narad felt compassionate and asked Jayant to only take refuge of Lord Ram. Whilst Jayant ran fearfully to take Ram's shelter, he kept his nervous gaze on the arrow, which was chasing after him. With his back to Lord Ram, still looking at the weapon, Jayant fell to the ground, his legs pointing towards Lord Ram. Lord Ram quietly watched Jayant's anguish, but the compassionate Sita guided Jayant to turn and bow his head at

[45] Jayant is the son of Indra (the king of the material heavens).

the lotus feet of Lord Ram. Thereafter, Lord Ram blessed Jayant and saved him from the weapon.

Likewise, great souls offer their compassion to people who feel hopeless with the frustrations of this material world. When one's home catches fire, all the neighbours come to help. In the same way, when people are burning in the fire of this material world, great souls bless these fortunate persons with their grace.

The material world is like a burning forest fire of misery caused by the elements, by other beings or by one's own mind. Forest fires can be caused by friction between the vines and trees. Similarly, the burning fire of material existence is caused simply by the friction between different material wants in the hearts of those who are influenced by desires. Moreover, when forest fires ignite, trees and vines cannot protect themselves. They either wait to burn to the ground or they wait until rainclouds come and shower water. Equally, the souls who are in the inferno of the material world have no means to free themselves from this burning; not until they receive the grace of great souls who come and impart the nectar of Lord Krishn's love. "There is no way to attain devotion other than the mercy of the great devotees. Forget attaining Krishn, without their mercy one cannot cross the ocean of life at all." (*Chaitanya Charitamrit*)

The grace of a great soul is compulsory, even if one has the grace of the Lord, and the following *Srimad Bhagwatam* quote (9.4.66) mentions this: "The sages control Me with their devotion, just as a loving wife controls a worthy husband." Those who have money can give money, and those who have ample food can offer food. Likewise, great souls are imbued with sacred love, and by their grace, aspirants have an opportunity to attain love, which can make aspirants achieve devotion. Lord Krishn Himself states, "I can be attained only through one-pointed faith and devotion." (*Srimad Bhagwatam* 11.14.21)

Finally, in this aphorism, Sage Narad mentions "through a little grace of the Lord." Why is there a need to mention the Lord's grace when one can achieve devotion by the grace of great souls? An aspirant is not able to encounter a great soul without the mercy of the Lord. When one gets ready to travel to a new country, one must abide by the direction of the expert who knows the way. Similarly, when a person craves for spiritual guidance and reaches out to the Lord to show him the way, Lord Krishn sends His divine grace in the form of a *guru*. The Lord does not shower His grace on everyone. He exercises choice in the matter and one needs to be sufficiently ready to receive this grace. For example if the will[46] is not there in a person to better himself, the combined will of others, who want to help him, can do nothing for him. Similarly, the Lord waits for that moment when the aspirant understands the goal of life. Once the Lord determines that the aspirant is ready, He bestows His grace only through the spiritual masters. The impact of this grace can be effectively experienced when the aspirant is able to understand its significant nature and when he sincerely follows his spiritual master's instructions.

---

[46] Will describes the act of strongly wanting to make something happen or having the hope to make it happen.

Sutra 39

|| *mahatsaṅgastu durlabho'gamyo'moghaśca* ||

The association of great souls is rarely obtained and recognized, yet it is infallible.

The *Srimad Bhagwatam* (11.12.1-2) describes the benefits of association: "Neither *yog*, nor intellectual analysis, nor austerity, nor scriptural study, nor renunciation, nor social service can bring the Lord under control as the company of true devotees can."

Once, Sage Vishvamitra asked Sage Vashisth about the glory of devotee association. Vashisth confessed his ignorance but took Vishvamitra to the Serpent King Balram, the most intimate devotee of the Lord, who at the time was bearing the whole Earth on his head to prevent it from falling. Balram said he was happy to reveal the glories of devotee association, if someone was able to take the burden of bearing this weight from him. Vishvamitra offered the fruit of all the austerities he had performed for thousands of years to the Lord, in return for strength to relieve Balram of his duty. When Earth was transferred to Vishvamitra's head, the sage found he was unable to endure it even for a small fraction of time. He immediately transferred it back to Balram.

Thereafter, Sage Vashisth offered the entire fruit of his present association, the noble company of Balram, to Krishn Himself. The planet nestled on his head firmly and with ease. At the request of Vishvamitra, Balram happily explained to Vishvamitra that he had just experienced the power of devotee association. The austerities Vishvamitra had performed for thousands of years could not rival the benediction received from the shortest time spent in the association of a pure devotee. "The value of a single moment's company with a devotee of the Lord is incomparable to the pleasure of the material heavens or liberation, what to speak of worldly pleasures." (*Srimad Bhagwatam* 1.18.13)

The first portion of this aphorism, "The association of great souls is rarely obtained . . . ," can have two meanings. Great souls are rare in this world. Vallabhacharya was a spiritual master and the founder of the *Pushtimarg* school of *Vaishnavism*. Once, a devotee approached him and told Vallabhacharya that he desired to feed a hundred *Brahmins*. Vallabhacharya replied that feeding one devotee equated to the result of feeding a hundred *Brahmins*.

"Then I want to feed a hundred devotees," the devotee replied.

Vallabhacharya said, "If you were to feed one *Brahmin* devotee, you would get the fruit of feeding a hundred devotees."

"Then I want to feed a hundred *Brahmin* devotees," the devotee replied.

Vallabhacharya responded, "If you were to feed one pure devotee, you would receive blessings equal to feeding a hundred *Brahmin* devotees."

"Then I want to feed a hundred pure devotees," said the devotee.

Vallabhacharya started to cry and replied, "It is very hard to find a hundred pure devotees."

But at the same time, great souls are not so rare that one should lose all hope of finding them. It is really a question of being able to recognize them. One should not assume that great souls can only be found residing in secluded mountains or deep in remote forests. Great souls are everywhere, but this aphorism is specifically stating that their association is rarely attained because it is the nature of sinful men to find sin.

Once, a sage took a new spiritual aspirant, who was a photographer by profession, for a class on the pastimes of Krishn. After the class finished, the sage asked the aspirant what kind of thoughts came into his mind whilst taking the class. The aspirant replied that throughout the talk, he was trying to think of how he could capture the speaker's beauty. Here, the aspirant was so distracted by his photography that he lost the opportunity to receive the nectar.

An inclination towards devotion to the Lord blossoms only when one associates with the right devotees. There is always a danger that one may take the shelter of a spiritual guide who is not suitable. In this instance, Narad forewarns aspirants to choose the association of true devotees. Association of great souls gives *sad-gati*, which is translated by Jeev Goswami in the *Bhakti Sandarbh* (section 179): "The word *sad* refers to the sages and *gati* means a vision of the Lord within the heart and mind. This means that the Lord manifests wherever sages gather. A tendency towards devotion is awakened in people who gather there, for the Lord appears wherever sages are found." Even though devotee association can give devotion, not all souls receive the benefits of this due to repeated offences committed by them.

Offences block the blessings from good association. Certain people repeatedly cause offences, and as a result, they become disrespectful towards devotees or consider them to be ordinary people. Even though the association of devotees has the power to centre people towards the awareness of the Lord, this counterproductive behaviour on the part of the person committing offences needs to be changed first.

Those who divert their minds away from the Lord by repeatedly committing offences are not eligible for the grace of devotees. The *Srimad Bhagwatam* (3.5.44) mentions those who are under the influence of offences: "The minds of those attracted to material pleasures roam aimlessly in the world. Such people cannot recognize those devotees who have realised Your sweetness, thus they remain far from Your lotus feet."

In a conversation with Maitreya, Vidur says, "Blessed devotees of Lord Krishn, like you, wander about in the world just to bless people who are sinful and suffering because of lack of devotion to Him." (*Srimad Bhagwatam* 3.5.3)

Although there is a difference between the two previous *Srimad Bhagwatam* verses, where (3.5.44) mentions that the great devotees do not forgive those who offend and (3.5.3) which states that pure devotees even bless those unfortunate persons who are not devoted to the Lord, the second verse is speaking about those who are unaware that they causing offences, therefore they are eligible for second chances. Whereas the offenders from verse (3.5.44) are the ones who know they are causing offences and continue to do so. These persons do not qualify to receive blessings from the great souls.

The *Srimad Bhagwatam* (11.2.29) states, "The human body is difficult to attain, and it can be destroyed at any moment. But it is even rarer to attain the association of great souls." Therefore, it is difficult for a person to recognize and associate with a great soul. Association does not necessarily mean physical association. Mere physical association of devotees cannot help anyone. Sages roam everywhere and they can be found residing in the holy places, along with many other great souls. Non-devotees, who also live there, come into contact with these enlightened devotees all the time, but one can question how much of this interaction develops into a communion with them.

In simple terms, if a person feels unhealthy, he may want to see a good doctor in his city of residence. He may need to see many doctors every day. To treat his disease, he needs to take guidance from a good doctor and receive treatment. Sometimes, to further improve his recovery process, he needs to change doctors after treatment has commenced. The path of spiritual aspiration is very much like this. One needs to remove idleness and approach the appropriate enlightened soul because devotion to the Lord makes the heart healthier and taking refuge of an elevated devotee can guide one directly to Him.

A man who continues to sleep after sunrise remains in the darkness of the night until he awakes. Here, the sunrise is an analogy for the association of great souls. In certain cases, this association does not have an immediate effect, therefore a man continues to sleep and remains in the dark, but he cannot remain in this state indefinitely. Once an aspirant gets the association of great devotees, he definitely attains their mercy, and in time, by the potency of this mercy, he will awaken because this aphorism describes the effect of holy company as "infallible."

Sutra 40

|| *labhyate'pi tatkṛpayaiva* ||

Association of great souls can be obtained through the Lord's grace alone.

The *Ramcharitmanas* (5.6.4) mentions, "One cannot get the company of the great souls without the Lord's grace." A story from the *Srimad Bhagwatam* illustrates this nicely. Stung by the harsh words of his stepmother, Dhruv left home to roam the forest for the purpose of performing austerities. Sage Narad met him on the way and gave him initiation, and showed Dhruv a way to meet the Lord. In this case, the chance meeting was not such a coincidence at all. It was motivated by the grace and compassion of the Lord because Dhruv had a deep yearning to meet Him.

The *Bhaktirasamrtasindhu* (1.3.16-20) elaborates on the concept of grace: "The grace of Krishn comes in three ways: through the voice, through vision and through the heart." Shankaracharya said, "Only by the grace of the Lord can we obtain the three rarest opportunities in the Universe: birth as a human being, the desire to attain freedom from the cycle of birth and death and discipleship to a realised teacher."

Therefore, the divine power of the Lord within an aspirant makes him impatient and genuinely active in his search for a great soul. At the same time, this divinity is also the driving force which makes great souls restless to offer their services for the devotion of others.

Sutra 41

|| *tasmiṁstajjane bhedābhāvāt* ||

Because the Lord and His great devotees are non-different.

In this aphorism, Sage Narad explains that without the association of great souls it is difficult to attain the Lord, and one cannot meet these great souls without the His grace.

A story from the *Mahabharat* illustrates the Lord's sentiment towards His great devotees. One day King Yuddhishthir went to see Lord Krishn, who was sitting on His bed, eyes closed, in a meditative pose. King Yuddhishthir stood before Him for some time. When Lord Krishn came out of His meditation, Yuddhishthir asked about the Lord's object of contemplation. Lord Krishn replied, "My great devotee Bhishma was meditating upon Me and I, upon him."

When an aspirant attains the level of devotion mentioned in the following *Srimad Bhagwatam* verse (9.4.68), "My loving devotees are My heart and I am their Heart. They know nothing but Me and I know none but them," he is adored by the Lord and being in the association of such an elevated devotee is non-different from being in the association of the Lord. The grace bestowed upon aspirants by a holy man is none other than the grace of the Lord. Hence, great souls and the Lord Himself are non-different from each other.

Therefore, Krishn says, "They[47] did not study the *Veds* nor did they ritualistically serve the saints. They did not perform vows or meditation either. Just by the effect of My devotees' association, they got Me." (*Srimad Bhagwatam* 11.12.7)

---

[47] They are the great devotees such as the *gopis*, Shabri, and so forth.

Sutra 42

|| *tadeva sādhyatāṁ tadeva sādhyatām* ||

Therefore without fail, attain that holy association alone.

Sage Narad glorifies the importance and potency of holy association. Thereafter, he instructs the aspirant to take holy association. Love is attained only through the company of pure devotees, which can advance an aspirant on his spiritual journey. "Powerful aspirants are unable to attain Me through *yog*, *Sankhya*, charity, vows, austerities, fire offerings, study of the *Veds* or renunciation. But by the association of My devotees, I can be attained easily." (*Srimad Bhagwatam* 11.12.9)

Therefore Krishn says, "Across the ages, countless souls have attained Me simply by keeping company with My devotees." (*Srimad Bhagwatam* 11.12.13)

In this aphorism, Sage Narad insists that pursuit of holy association is essential if one wants to taste the sweetness of devotion, and in search of such association, one should not waste a precious moment.

Sutra 43

|| *duḥsaṅgaḥ sarvathaiva tyājyaḥ* ||

One should avoid bad association of any kind.

One may use separate water to bathe in and to drink, and there are still other types of water that are not fit for use. Similarly, there are many kinds of association that can nourish or harm spiritual life. On the path of devotion, Sage Narad cautions aspirants to avoid bad company.

> When a water droplet hits a hot iron, it evaporates and leaves no trace; a water droplet falling on a lotus leaf nestles there and gleams like a pearl; and when a raindrop falls on an oyster shell during the period of *Swaati*,[48] it becomes a real pearl. In the same way, one attains basic, mediocre or superior attributes according to the company one keeps. (*Nitishatakam*, verse 68)

Whilst Narad advises against bad association, he does not instruct an aspirant to disconnect himself from civilisation. However, there are many spiritual masters who push their aspirants to initially disconnect from worldly contact, which is extremely hard to do in practice. Sometimes, it becomes difficult for new aspirants to detach from the material world and its people and only absorb themselves into the spiritual world. The spiritual masters are not necessarily misguiding devotees with this teaching because the practice of devotion should help one remember the Lord uninterruptedly. However, in the beginning, it would be more appropriate to instruct one to detach oneself from the negative aspects of worldly life. In the next aphorism, Sage Narad clarifies what constitutes bad association.

---

[48] *Swaati* is a star in *Vedic* astrology.

Sutra 44

|| *kāma krodha moha smṛtibhraṁśabuddhināśa sarvanāśa kāraṇatvāt* ||

Bad association brings lust, anger, delusion, forgetfulness of the goal and complete ruin.

In this aphorism, Sage Narad reveals the qualities of bad association. One who comes into contact with negative association experiences increased levels of lust, anger, delusion, and so forth. Therefore, one should be very wary of keeping such company.

> By paying attention to the things which are attractive to the senses, one becomes attached to those things. From attachment, desire comes, and from desire comes anger. From anger comes delusion, from delusion confusion and from confusion comes the loss of the ability to think logically, which in turn leads to one's ruin. (*Bhagwad Gita* 2.62-63)

In his commentary on the preceding verses, Keshav Kashmiri wrote:

> Lord Krishn states that he who dwells on form, touch and other sensual stimuli, develops attachment for them in his heart, having become deluded into thinking those material objects are capable of giving him real permanent happiness. From this attachment comes desire, which is merely a mutation of attachment. Sometimes he feels some satisfaction by indulging in enjoyment of these sense objects.

When enjoyment of objects that attract the senses results in pleasure, a state of mind arises whereby one becomes controlled by the very same object that one is desperately seeking to exploit (in other words, one becomes a slave to the sense objects). Sometimes, a person cannot attain the object of his desire and he experiences frustration, which is also simply a mutation of the state of mind. When this happens, a person's anger is directed towards whatever stands between him and the fulfilment of his wants. From anger comes delusion or the lack of the ability to discriminate between what should and should not be done.

When there is confusion in one's ability to reason and when one forgets the wisdom from the scriptures, as instructed by spiritual masters, one becomes deluded. Delusion is the mind's misinterpretation of the true nature of reality. When a person interprets reality without wisdom, he starts acting to fulfil his desires and lusts and he loses focus on the goal and purpose of life. Thus, he becomes lost in the oblivion of ignorance. Therefore, control of the mind is essential.

An aspirant may feel he is strong enough not to be influenced by the company he keeps. Sage Narad discourages this attitude. Perhaps, initially, the aspirant tolerates the bad effect of negative association. With the effects of continual exposure, he will become vulnerable, and later, he himself will take on the negative qualities of others. Just as good company inspires sacred love, bad association awakens lust, anger, and so forth.

When a young tree flourishes, she needs protection from stray animals, but when she is fully grown, she gives fruit and shelter to all. In the same manner, an advanced aspirant on the path of devotion is barely affected by negative company. However, in one's spiritual journey, protection from bad company is a necessity.

Sutra 45

|| *taraṅgayitā apīme saṅgāt samudrāyanti* ||

In the beginning, these passions may remain like ripples but bad association turns them into an ocean.

One who really desires devotion should hold the objects of sense enjoyment at a distance and joyfully continue drinking the nectar of good virtues, such as contentment, compassion, forgiveness and self-control. Each person has elements of good and bad in him. The nature of association provokes either good or bad qualities within a person and makes them better or worse. The negative symptoms arising from bad association can be a hurdle or a hindrance in the aspirant's devotional life. Sage Narad urges the devotee to keep far from the fire of bad company, because lust and anger cannot be controlled within these environments. One should not become complacent and believe that one is strong enough not to be affected by such powerful influences. Carelessness may lead to ruin. "It would be a greater calamity to live amongst people averse to remembering Lord Krishn than to dwell in a cage in the midst of a raging inferno." (*Chaitanya Charitamrit* 2.22.91)

6

Overcoming Delusion

Sutra 46

|| kastarati kastarati māyāṁ? yaḥ saṅgāṁtyajati yo mahānubhāvaṁ sevate nirmamo bhavati ||

Who overcomes delusion? He who gives up all attachment, he who serves great souls and he who gives up the idea of egotism.

Here, delusion refers to the ignorance that keeps an aspirant distant from reality. The Lord Himself confirms in the *Bhagwad Gita* (7.25), "I do not reveal Myself to everyone but keep Myself veiled by My Yogmaya.[49] Thus, those bereft of wisdom cannot recognize Me as the eternal Lord."

The first part of the aphorism states, "Who overcomes delusion? He who gives up all attachment . . . ." Therefore, Sage Narad states some qualities that the aspirant needs to acquire in order to remove this delusion. These qualities have been discussed previously, but in this aphorism, Narad mentions them to strengthen his point.

One who wants to swim across a river must use one's arms and legs constantly against the water pressure, to push through the water. A beginner can eventually cross a river by performing this repetitive action, but the moment he stops swimming he will surely drown. Likewise, he who has a desire to cross the river of delusion has to persistently contend against his egoism, and see through worldly attachments, which make the water murky. One who is not resilient will surely sink into its bottomless depth.

Swimming across a river for a beginner may feel tiring, and he may need regular breaks to rest his limbs. Similarly, constantly swimming

[49] Yogmaya is the goddess who creates various kinds of (positive) confusion in the world or in the Lord's abode for various purposes in the course of the Lord's divine play.

in the river of ignorance can exhaust an aspirant and he may take a step back and find himself in the beneficial position of contemplation, giving him an opportunity to restore his energy and fight back. For example, the aspirant may abandon his devotional practice for some time. Absolute renunciation from attachments cannot help a devotee initially; he must allow time for his spiritual evolution.

Thus, in the second part of the aphorism, Narad advises one to take the necessary intervals by serving great souls. However, serving does not necessarily imply living in the company of saints or rendering physical service to them, although in one's devotional practice such service is essential and advisable when one is fortunate enough to be in this position. It is most important to follow the teachings of a spiritual master. If an aspirant acts according to his own instructions by not following the teachings and regulates his life according to his limited understanding, his service will be regarded as flawed by the scriptures. A devotee who enjoys the privilege of true service to the great souls crosses the river of delusion effortlessly. The grace of the great souls comes and ferries him across. Therefore, Narad advises the aspirant to take to the service of these elevated beings. The *Srimad Bhagwatam* (11.26.32) states, "My peaceful, saintly devotees are the only lifeboat for those tossed by waves of the terrible ocean of material life."

Lochan Das Thakur, one of the earliest biographers of Chaitanya Mahaprabhu, wrote the following song:

ke jābi ke jābi bhāi bhavasindhu pār
dhanya kalijuger chaitanya avatār
āmār gaurāṅger ghāṭe adān-kheyā boy
jaḍa, andha, ātur avadhi pār hoy
harināmer naukākhāni śri guru kāṇḍārī
sankīrtan kheroyāl dubāhu pasāri
sab jīv hoila pār premer vātāse
paḍiyā rahila lochan āpanār doṣe

> "'Oh brothers! Who will go? Who will go across the ocean of misery? In this blessed *Kaliyug*, Lord Chaitanya has come! At my Gaurang's[50] *ghat*[51] a boat is waiting. The ignorant, blind, and distressed - all shall be ferried across. That boat is the Holy Name of Krishn, Sri *Guru* is the captain. The *Sankirtan*[52] party rows it with their upraised arms as oars.'

---

[50] Gaurang is one of Chaitanya Mahaprabhu's names.

[51] A *ghat* is a wide flight of steps leading to Indian riverbank.

[52] *Sankirtan* is the collective singing of the Lord's Names.

> Thus all souls were taken across, propelled by the wind of sacred love. Only I, the poet Lochan, was left behind, on account of all my faults."

One's relationship with the world can become an obstacle in one's service to great souls. Possessive feelings for worldly objects prevent the aspirants from serving the saints. Hence, Narad gives light to further knowledge in the third part of the aphorism "who gives up the idea of egotism." Once an aspirant removes his ego, he receives the necessary devotional mood and association. As an example, when a man checks into a hotel room, he does not feel that the room is his home. When a person eats at a restaurant, he does not feel that it is his kitchen and dining room. With the same mood, one should take this Earth as a hotel and use its resources, but one must eliminate the feeling of ownership towards them, which is the root of possessiveness. Without this practice, the desire to possess more will awaken, binding one into a never-ending cycle of chasing after those wants.

Sutra 47

|| yo viviktasthānaṁ sevate yo lokabandhamunmūlayati nistraiguṇyo bhavati yo yogakṣemaṁ tyajati ||

Who can overcome delusion? He who lives in solitude, cuts off the bondages of this world, goes beyond the three qualities of nature and renounces the idea of obtaining or preserving the objects of the world.

The *Bhagwad Gita* (13.10) states, "Do your devotional practice with dedication and live in a holy place, away from materialistic people." Spiritual masters who have written many commentaries on this aphorism have said that Sage Narad is instructing aspirants to cut off all worldly relations and live in solitude. These remarks imply that Sage Narad is contradicting himself by advising all spiritual aspirants to attain holy association and also recommending a life of isolation.

The *Srimad Bhagwatam* recounts the tale of a young girl whose family were interviewing suitors for her marriage. One day, while she was home alone, a prospective groom and his family came to her house. The maiden had to carry the whole burden of entertaining them. While she was cooking, her bracelets jingled. Fearing her guests would be disturbed, she took off her bangles one by one till only two remained on each wrist. When those two bangles still made noise, she took another off each hand leaving only one. Then she was able to do her work in silence. The *Srimad Bhagwatam* concludes that one should therefore live alone, for the sake of peace in spiritual practice.

However, the commentator Vishwanath Chakravarti Thakur explains that this instruction is meant for followers of the path of knowledge. The path of devotion is different. Bhakti Devi is a queen who wears many colourful bangles to please her Husband. And her Husband is pleased to hear the jingling of her bangles when she runs into His arms and embraces Him. Therefore, in this world, Bhakti Devi brings devotees together so that they can please the Lord with the joyful tumult of *sankirtan*.

Thus, Sage Narad does not mean one must live in seclusion throughout one's life. Living under these extreme conditions, the aspirant is in danger of becoming egotistical. In fact, the aphorisms begin by establishing that the path of devotion is for everyone, including householders, merchants, businessmen and students.

Under these circumstances, it is not possible for these groups of people to completely cut connections with their relations and live in seclusion.

Some aspirants leave their households, where their minds remain disturbed and prevent them from any devotional practice, and choose to reside in solitary places. Some delude themselves into thinking that they are rid of all worldly attachments such as friends, family, money, and so forth, and that their renunciation is fully mature. Other aspirants argue with family members and as an act of rebellion, they leave their homes. Such aspirants will not succeed because they will carry their dissatisfaction, bitterness and wounded egos wherever they go. In one's sincere efforts to tread the path of devotion, misunderstanding this aphorism can lead to failure.

Hence, Sage Narad recommends occasional solitude for the aspirant. Whilst living in seclusion, a devotee can completely devote himself to the Lord. The absence of connections to the mundane world enables the devotee to hear and sing the Lord's glories and meditate upon Him. Isolation does not have to entail leaving home and family. One can simply set aside time and space for exclusively connecting to the Lord. Saint Ramkrishna said:

> If you wish to make butter, you must curdle the milk and leave it in a place where it will remain undisturbed. If someone disturbs it, the curd will not stand. Then, if you churn it, butter will rise from your churning. Similarly, the aspirant should sit in quiet solitude, where no one can disturb him. Then, when he churns his heart through meditation and spiritual practice, the butter of sacred love will arise. If you give your heart and mind to the Lord in peace and solitude, you will attain true renunciation and devotion. But if you give your heart and mind to the world, you will attain only worldliness. You will become increasingly filled with greed and desire.
>
> The world is like water, the heart like milk. When water and milk are mixed together, both liquids cannot be separated. But if the heart is transformed into the butter of sacred love through spiritual practice, it separates from the water and can be extracted. When that state comes, never again shall the heart mix in the water of worldliness. Instead, it shall rise above materialism, and though remaining in the world, it shall simultaneously remain totally separate. Thus having attained sacred love for the Lord and real understanding of

> who He is, one dwells in the world as one who is completely separate.

When a fruit becomes mature and ripe, it falls and separates itself from the tree. Once the need for true renunciation is felt, the aspirant cuts off his worldly bondages. If one cuts off his connections prematurely, then social obligations such as taking care of family members and attending marriages and funerals, as well as a number of other duties, will disturb one's life of solitude. Once the aspirant becomes mature, he realises that his family is not just limited to his material relations. The whole world becomes his family because the aspirant sees the Lord in everyone, and without discrimination, he serves them all with great humility.

To eliminate delusion, the aspirant is required to go beyond the threefold qualities of nature. In the fourteenth chapter of the *Bhagwad Gita,* Lord Krishn explains these three qualities (*gunas*) clearly:

1. *Sattva*: The quality of purity, mental stillness and clarity
2. *Rajas*: The quality of passion, activity and restlessness
3. *Tamas*: The quality of ignorance and inertia

These three qualities of nature exist in combinations and in different quantities within each individual, and he or she will act according to the quality that is most prominent in him or her. *Sattva* is a quality which makes a person search for happiness and worldly awareness. *Rajas* is a quality which makes a person lusty, greedy and bound by habitual activities. *Tamas* is a quality which makes one foolish, lazy and weak. Therefore in the *Bhagwad Gita* (14.22-25), Krishn says:

> One who does not get upset by material purity, passion, or delusion when they are present nor yearn for them when they are absent; who remains focused and undisturbed through all life's changes, which are caused by the interaction of the three material qualities; who is always engrossed in the bliss of the soul and accepts pleasure and pain alike; who sees a clump of earth, a rock and a piece of gold as equal; who accepts both compliments and criticism in the same spirit; who is the same in pleasant or unpleasant circumstances; who treats friends and enemies equally and who does not consider oneself the accomplisher of actions, can be understood to have passed beyond the three qualities.

Lord Krishn concludes by saying, "One who worships Me by the path of devotion goes beyond the three qualities and becomes fit to attain *Brahman*." (*Bhagwad Gita* 14.26)

The final requirement for removing delusion is renunciation of the idea of obtaining or preserving material objects. There can be two forms of desires that arise in the heart and mind. Sometimes a person acquires some precious objects that he wants to preserve, and occasionally he tries to obtain objects that he does not have. Thus, Narad advises the aspirant to renounce the idea of obtaining and preserving any object, because one who has completely surrendered to the Lord needs to only depend on Him.

Sutra 48

|| *yaḥ karmaphalaṁ tyajati karmāṇi sannyasyati tato nirdvandvo bhavati* ||

Who can overcome delusion? He who gives up the effect of all actions. He who renounces all actions passes beyond duality, such as pleasure and pain, and so forth.

"Nobody can stop acting for even one moment, for all beings are constantly compelled by the three qualities, as a result of their past actions." (*Bhagwad Gita* 3.5)

In his commentary on this verse, Madhvacharya said:

> The point being made here is that it is impossible to renounce every single action. In the *Paingi Shruti*, action is divided into two categories. The two kinds of action are: action which has a cause and action dependent of any external cause. The actions dependent on a cause occur by the influence of the three qualities of nature. Causeless action is that which is made to happen by the Lord.

Each thought and every action results in either happiness or misery. This aphorism refers to the activities of self-interest and by no means suggests that one should become lazy or inactive and give up action or stop thinking. When one performs a task, one expects something in return. This is an attachment to the fruit of the doer's action and if he receives the desired reward, he becomes happy, otherwise misery transpires in him. The performance of such actions and attachment to the results disturb the mind of the aspirant and consequently divert his meditation away from the Lord. "It is your right only to perform action. You have no control over the results of your actions. Do not see yourself as the cause of the results, but do not become attached to inaction either." (*Bhagwad Gita* 2.47)

Desire is the anticipation of a reward. Consequently, those who possess spiritual intelligence should not be motivated by the incentive behind performing an action. Action motivated by desire for reward warrants reaction and therefore binds one to material bondage. The performance of austerities, without the hope of obtaining a result, is the means of overcoming these yearnings. Desireless actions performed as a matter of duty are full of wisdom.

Therefore, the wise are not bound by desire for rewards. Even if one is unable to prevent desire, Lord Krishn advises:

> All that you give, all that you eat, all that you place in the fire as an offering, all that you endure - all that you do, do everything as an offering for Me. By doing so, you will become free from the good and bad results of your actions and you will attain Me. (*Bhagwad Gita* 9.27-28)

Therefore, to prevent an aspirant from feeling the effects of results, to free him from the cycle of pain and pleasure and to help him rise above delusion, Sage Narad advises renunciation. In the *Bhagwad Gita* (18.11), Lord Krishn states, "Anyone whose soul is in a body cannot stop acting completely. But one who renounces attachment to the results of one's actions can rightly be called a renounced person." Lord Krishn explains that it is impossible for any living entity to completely renounce actions and the cessation of activities alone is not renunciation. Actual renunciation takes place when the desire for rewards of actions and one's ego is relinquished.

Sutra 49

|| *yo vedānapi sannyasyati kevalamavicchinnānurāgaṁ labhate* ||

Who can overcome delusion? He who discards the *Veds* and attains uninterrupted love for the Lord.

The aspirant should discard the *Veds*, advises Sage Narad. Although initially seeming controversial, the following *Srimad Bhagwatam* verse indicates the reason: "Brahma examined the *Veds* thrice over, and after deeply pondering the matter, determined the ultimate process to be that which brings about the attainment of sacred love by the soul." (*Srimad Bhagwatam* 2.2.34)

When the *Veds* speak about Lord Krishn, it may be difficult to understand Narad's reasons for opposing them. In the *Bhagwad Gita* (2.42-44), Lord Krishn's dialogue with Arjun supports Narad's opposition:

> O Arjun! Men desiring enjoyment love the flowery language of the *Veds*. They look upon the pleasure-gardens of the gods as the supreme goal. If they get carried away by hopes for pleasure and power, they become deeply attached to those hopes and thus cannot attain the determination needed to concentrate on the Lord.

Those who want to attain the lotus feet of the Lord through one-pointed devotional practice, serving Him only, may be distracted by the ritualistic portions of the *Veds*. Sense satisfaction resulting from these ceremonies, in this life or the next, can lead to further entanglement. Therefore, it is better to give them up. The essence of the *Veds* is to enhance an aspirant's spiritual progress and not to hinder it. In his commentary on the *Bhagwad Gita* verses (2.42-44), Keshav Kashmiri states:

> Those addicted to sensory pleasures are overwhelmingly attracted by the extravagant promises of the *Veds* to the point of distraction. Their minds are thus rendered unfit to conceive of and meditate upon the Lord; they are unable to perceive and realise Him. They are unable to attain one-pointed focus because they lack the proper wisdom and understanding, and this they lack because they perform no acts of loving devotion for the Lord.

At the same time, one cannot turn away from the instructions of the *Veds* because they have their place on the path of devotion. "One who desires to quickly cut the knot of the heart, which seals the soul in bondage, should offer loving worship to Krishn according to the rites described in the *Veds* and the *Tantra*."[53] (*Srimad Bhagwatam* 11.3.47)

To illustrate this point, a person uses his car to reach a friend's home. The moment he arrives at his destination, the car is left in the drive and not taken inside the house. The instructions within the *Veds* carry the aspirant up to a certain point in his devotional practice and thereafter, to taste the nectar of devotion, one must go beyond them. The *Srimad Bhagwatam* (4.29.46) declares the same: "When a devotee receives the Lord's mercy, he loses all preoccupation with worldly life as well as the ritualism of the *Veds*."

---

[53] *Tantra* is a practice of religious rituals written in the scriptures.

Sutra 50

|| *sa tarati sa tarati sa lokāṁstārayati* ||

He crosses over, certainly he crosses over. He even helps others cross over their delusion.

By following the ten subsequent instructions from aphorism 46 to 49 with conviction, one dispels one's delusion:

1. Renounce all attachment
2. Serve the great souls
3. Let go of ego
4. Live in solitude
5. Break the bonds of worldliness
6. Rise above the threefold qualities of the material world
7. Renounce the idea of obtaining or preserving the objects of the world
8. Give up the results of all actions
9. Renounce all actions and pass beyond the pairs of opposites
10. Discard the *Veds*

Sage Narad assures that those who abide by these instructions will surely rise above delusion; they will even help others to surpass it.

7

Sacred Love

Sutra 51

|| *anirvacanīyaṁ premasvarūpam* ||

The nature of love is beyond words; it is indescribable.

In the previous aphorisms, Sage Narad described the nature of delusion. Here, he says that once a seeker crosses the world of delusion, he attains sacred love (*prem*), which is indescribable. Sacred love is the topmost goal of a living being and devotion is the means to obtain this love. The *Gaudiya Sampradaya*, the Chaitanya School of *Vaishnavism*, reveals the different processes to reach the level where one experiences sacred love:

> First comes acquisition of faith by the company of devotees, then learning the process of *bhajan* (sweet remembrance whilst performing any action) from them. Thereafter, the practice of *bhajan* begins, which leads to *anartha-nivritti* (cessation of harmful habits and cleansing of bad qualities), *nistha* (steadiness in *bhajan*), *ruchi* (consistent delight in every item of practice), *asakti* (deep attachment), *bhaav* (extreme maturity of *asakti*) and then *prem* (sacred love). This is the general sequence in which the spiritual development of the aspirant occurs. (*Bhaktirasamrtasindhu* 1.4.15-16)

When a devotee feels very intense longing for Lord Krishn, it is called sacred love. Gopal Bhatt Goswami, a disciple of Chaitanya Mahaprabhu, explains in his *Krishn Karnamrit* commentary:

> Sacred love is the only means by which we can see Lord Krishn. Without sacred love, even if we meet Him, it is as if we have not met Him. When He manifested Himself on Earth, even demons saw Him but they could not relish a single drop of the ocean of joy that He is. Instead, they burned with anger, envy and violence. Thus we can

understand that sacred love is the only way to relish Lord Krishn's sweetness.

The nectar of sacred love is not dependent on words, actions, caste, creed, colour or on relationships. One may say that love is happiness, yet one finds that sadness is also a part of love. For instance, when a bride leaves to join her husband's family, after the happy occasion of a wedding ceremony, her own family cries. This crying is due to love and not due to worldly suffering.

One may say that love is service to others. This is not true either because the servitor can enjoy the act of serving others but not actually fulfil their needs. In his bliss, he may feel that the ones he is serving are also in that state of joy. To illustrate, Vishwambhar Goswami, from the Radharaman Temple in Vrindavan, described the following situation; once a disciple asked his secretary, "How can I please my spiritual master Vishvambhar Goswami?"

"Goswamiji always accepts whatever is offered to him with love. He is drawn to love, like a bee to a bright flower. So serve him as much love as you can," the secretary replied.

When Vishvambhar Goswami went to the house of his disciple, he started feeding Goswamiji constantly and started massaging his legs without giving him rest. Shortly thereafter, Goswamiji started to get annoyed by the service. Therefore, love is not service alone.

There are a number of examples which prove that the sacred love experienced by a devotee cannot be limited by words. Thus Radha explains to her friend, "Listen, if you wish to know about sacred love. 'This is the extent of sacred love; it is like this, not like that.' One who understands sacred love in this way does not really understand it, though one may be a great scholar of the *Ved*." (*Prem Samput*, verse 51)

Love can make one cry or feel extreme happiness or extreme envy, yet love can also give freedom. Love is something that can be felt by the heart. Lord Ram sent a love message to His wife Sita, when She was held captive in Lanka:

tattva prem kar mam aru torā, jānat priyā eku manu morā
so manu sadā rahat tohi pāhiň jānu prīti rasu etanehi māhiň

"My Darling, only My heart knows the truth of Our love, and My heart always resides with You. Try to understand our

> relationship by this fact alone." (*Ramcharitmanas, Sundar Kand*)

Love is experienced by the heart and the heart of the lover stays with the Beloved. In the absence of the heart, words cannot describe the experiences of the lover, not even imperfectly. Therefore, the impression one attains of love is but a mere hint of its nature. A person who has taken a plunge into deep waters will find it impossible to speak until he resurfaces, and not even whilst he is swimming to the surface. In the same way, one who is submerged into the depth of the ocean of love finds oneself incapable of speaking.

ḍubai so bolai nahīň, bolai so anjān
gahrau prem samudra kou ḍubai chatur sujān

> "One who is deep under water cannot speak; one who speaks is a fool. The ocean of love is exceedingly deep. Only a wise soul can plunge to the bottom of it." (*Vrajwasi Poetry*)

Hence, Sage Narad says that the limitation of words cannot describe the ocean-like vast experience of sacred love; sacred love can only be experienced.

Sutra 52

|| *mūkāsvādanavat* ||

It is like the taste of the mute.

In this aphorism, Sage Narad very wisely explains the nature of sacred love. He says that sacred love is like a mute person's experience of taste. This can be understood by a simple example. If one gives pancakes, candies and chocolate to a mute person to eat and afterward asks him to describe the taste, he will not be able to do so. Even if the mute person tries to express it to another, the recipient cannot understand unless he himself has tasted those objects.

Love cannot be compared to chocolates, candies, the moon or the ocean. Love is beyond material comparison. Comparisons can only give a mere hint of the sweetness of love. That indescribable love is experienced by a lover only. Love is not expressible; it can only be understood by the person who has a similar kind of love. This point is further illustrated by the following tale. Once, a sage was walking through a forest and he found a Deity of the Lord resting inappropriately on the ground. So he made a suitable throne, placed the Deity on it and left. Another sage passing by felt that the throne should have a roof over it, to shelter the Deity from the rain and the intense rays of the sun. He came and built a thatched roof above the throne and left. After a few days, some other sages were passing through. They found the Deity, the throne and the roof and they felt that if there was a forest fire and if the roof caught on fire, it would harm the Deity. So they removed the roof. Though they contradicted each other externally, the reactions of all the sages equally expressed their love.

One even forgets oneself in love; the devotee forgets his identity and his knowledge in the joy of love, and in this blissful state, he is incapable of describing sacred love. Once, Radha said to Her friends that She knew nothing of Her love for Krishn; She understood nothing about it and if She understood anything at all, then She had no words to describe it. She only knew one thing: the moment She felt His touch, inside Her heart, She lost all consciousness.

Therefore sacred love cannot be defined nor can the expression of sacred love be categorised; sacred love can only be understood by lovers who have crossed over an ocean of delusion.

Sutra 53

|| *prakāśate' kvāpi pātre* ||

That sacred love appears in a worthy person.

In the 21st aphorism, Sage Narad compared sacred love to the love which the *gopis* had for Krishn and in this aphorism, Narad states that this love arises in one who is worthy. If one tries to hold the milk of a lioness in a clay pot, steel pot, iron pot, or even in a silver pot, the milk will spoil. It can only be held in a gold pot. Similarly, the highest stage of love can only be contained by a heart that is refined by serious spiritual practice. When a person connects his love with an impure object, the love turns into desire, yet when that person connects his love with the purest object (Lord Krishn), his lust or desires turn into sacred love:

premaiva goparāmāṇaṁ kāma itygamat pratham

> "The love of the *gopis* was criticized for being lusty but it was not, because it was not directed towards an impure object. Here, what could be perceived as their lust was actually love." (*Shridhar Swami*, *Bhaktirasamrtasindhu* 1.2.285)

The *Chaitanya Charitamrit* (1.4.172) also defends the reputation of the *gopis*: "The love of the cowherd girls of Vraj is totally pure, free from the stain of lust. They acted solely for the sake of Krishn's pleasure." When the Lord-loving-souls drink this sacred love, rays of love radiate from them: not only through the words and eyes of such souls but through every pore of their bodies. Such manifestation of sacred love is a direct revelation of the Lord Himself, which materialises in one who is worthy of this grace.

Sutra 54

|| *guṇarahitaṁ kāmanārahitaṁ pratikṣaṇa vardhamānaṁ avichhinnaṁ sūkṣmataramanubhavarūpam* ||

This sacred love is devoid of qualities, it is desireless and it increases with each moment. It is unbroken, is subtler than the subtlest and it is the form of innermost experience.

The Lord is described by the six main attributes He possesses: wealth, fame, strength, knowledge, beauty and detachment. Sacred love is a form of the Lord, and here, Sage Narad defines the six attributes of sacred love:

1. Devoid of qualities: The following incident was published in a Spanish newspaper. A beautiful woman, with long silky hair and beautiful teeth, used to visit a bar regularly. One night at the bar, a man, who found her very attractive, approached her and started to compliment her splendour by telling her how luscious her hair was, how beautiful her teeth were and how stunning she looked. Whenever she would go to the bar, the same man would approach her and praise her beauty again and again.

One evening, she asked him, "Do you really admire my beauty?"

"I have never known anyone as beautiful as you. You are the most gorgeous woman I have ever seen," he replied.

She said, "Come home with me."

They went to her house and they sat down, and she asked him, "Can you please tell me again how beautiful I am?"

"I never saw such long and silky hair. It seems like God created you with His own hands," he replied.

The woman took off her wig and said, "Seeing as you love my hair, let me give it to you and as you are very fond of my teeth as well, here, have them."

She pulled out her false teeth and gave them to him. Seeing her without teeth and hair, the man was stunned and speechless and he left the house silently. In this situation, the love was dependent on the qualities possessed by the woman and not the woman herself.

People tend to love because they are either attracted towards the beauty, power, money, intelligence, humility or any other kind of quality which they find attractive in the person they desire. But they love only as long as these qualities exist in them. Many relationships end because what one perceives as love is actually a love of the qualities which exist in one's partner and if those qualities fade or change with time or circumstances, the connection deteriorates. Sage Narad very clearly says that sacred love is devoid of qualities. One who pursues desires connected with the senses does so for self-satisfaction. Sacred love is not connected to the senses because without even seeing one's Beloved, without hearing about the Beloved, without touching the Beloved, the love still blossoms in one's heart.

Once, some friends asked Radha, "Why do You love Krishn even though He's a thief?"

Radha replied, "I know His heart. He does not want that we should be defamed, so He tries to act like a naughty child. He steals butter from various houses so His elders will feel that He is not mature enough to do any chores. By being mischievous, He gets ample free time and gets the chance to meet Me."

Radha loves Krishn regardless of his good or bad qualities. She loves Him for the sake of love and this is the first point of this aphorism.

2. Desireless: There is a slight difference between love and desire. A particular desire can be quenched, for example by buying an object one craves. The urge leaves once the object is bought, but when one feels love, the feeling intensifies with each moment and there is no definitive end to the experience. There is a story which illustrates the nature of desire. A street performer wanted to impress a king, in order to acquire the king's horse as a reward. So he sat in meditation and went into a deep trance. The king was really impressed and gave an order to his ministers to put him in a room. Time passed and the king died. Thereafter, a few generations passed, yet the street performer did not come out of his trance. One day, he emerged from his meditation and the first thing he said was, "Oh King! Are you impressed by my meditation? Will you reward me your horse?" Even after spending hundreds of years in meditation, his desire to own that horse was not satisfied.

Desire yearns to satisfy oneself, whereas love wants to satisfy one's beloved. There are two types of devotees: one who is desirous and one who loves. If both of these devotees offer food to their Deities, the one who desires will offer what he really wants to eat that day, according to his taste and wants his Lord to be pleased with his choice. Yet the loving one will try to find signs, try to feel and understand what Krishn Himself wants to eat that day. Loving someone with desire is love offered on the basis of conditions; it is one where the motive is of mutual pleasure, not exclusive pleasure for the Lord. In this case, the feeling of dissatisfaction remains within, whether one's desire is fulfilled or not. But love in its purest form loves the Beloved for His sake.

3. Sacred love increases with each moment: In India, the river Ganga starts from Gomukh. The Ganga emerges as a stream at the origin, and the more she flows, the more she increases in width. At the end, where she meets the sea, she is known as Ganga Sagar. Here, she is very wide. People say that the breadth of the Ganga River at Ganga Sagar is more than 40 kilometres. The nature of love is also like this; it expands with time.

A lover always feels that his love is inadequate, and this inspires a deep yearning in him to use every effort to increase the level of his affection towards his Beloved. This sentiment develops sacred love in him. From one day to the next, this pristine love grows rapidly.

prem sadā baṛhibau karai jyo sasikalā subeṣh
pai punau yāme nahī, tāte kabahu na seṣh

> "Sacred Love grows eternally like a waxing moon, but this moon is never full and its waxing never ends." (*Vrajwasi Poetry*)

4. It is an unbroken inner experience: Sacred love is never broken. There are people who show intense love, but as a result of jealousy or heartache, triggered by an action from their beloved, they end the relationship. Or they show anger and start to behave negatively and walk away. This is not the nature of sacred love. Sacred love is never broken, even if a lover hears something bad about his Lord. Once one starts to love Lord Krishn, it becomes difficult for even the Lord Himself to break that connection. For example, in the *Srimad Bhagwatam*, the *gopis* came to Krishn to take part in the *Raas Mandal,* and He asked them to go back to their houses, but they refused. By this instruction, Lord Krishn was testing how eager the *gopis* were to be with Him, and when they melted His heart with their unflinching devotion to Him, He accepted them into the *Raas Mandal*. He did not break the devotional connection that the *gopis* had started.

Many canals originate from a river. In the beginning these canals are very broad, but they trail off before reaching the ocean. The same can be said about people who show intense love in the beginning but whose love fades with time and without reaching the ocean of sacred love. In the devotional world, there is one type of devotee who is like a river; his love always increases and is never broken. Equally, there is another type of devotee whose love can be compared to a flowing canal. He shows so much love in the beginning but when he finds that his desires are not fulfilled by the Lord or when he does not find his desired connection with the Lord, he feels like he is wasting his time in the relationship. Sacred love is not like this. It is an unbroken chain which connects one to the Lord with the mood of complete devotion and without any preconceptions or expectations.

5. Subtler than the subtlest: Once the *gopis* asked Brahma, "Please transform us into divine dust of Vraj so that a potter may collect it and make a clay cup for Krishn, and maybe Krishn will fill the cup with water or milk and kiss it with His beautiful lips. We know that it is hard for us to be with Him but by becoming subtle like Vraj dust we can be with Him always." A lover tries to be in his Beloved's service in every way. He does not try to present his offering as a gesture to impress his Lord. The lover just tries to be at his Lord's service and endeavours to make Him happy.

6. Form of innermost experience: There is a difference between knowledge and love. In love, even if the beloved is physically far away, the lover experiences that his beloved is present with him. The nature of this relationship is such that even if the couple have disagreements or see flaws in each other, it does not impact the love they feel for each other or their experience of that love. The love transforms the beloved's imperfection into perfection. This affection even keeps the beloved alive when he or she is physically deceased. But when one is drawn to the path of knowledge, one feels the actual reality. If someone is physically far, he is far. If someone is not beautiful, he is not beautiful and if someone is dead, he is dead. The nature of love has the power to make a stranger into one's dearest. The particle *bhav* in the word *anubhav* means that which changes constantly. The *anu* particle transforms the meaning of *bhav* into: that which never changes. And love is *anubhav*, that innermost experience. Everything changes over the course of one's life such as one's body, religion, relationships, and so forth, but what remains unchanged is *anubhav*: one's innermost experience with the Lord.

Once, one of the closest associates of Radha, Lalita, asked Her, "What is the nature of Your relationship with Krishn?"

Radha replied, "Whatever you feel defines Our relationship, give it that name." Her response showed that a relationship is not bound by a name. All relationships are dependent on love, but love is not dependent on relationships.

Lalita replied, "You are His Beloved and He is Your Beloved."

Radha replied, "O friend! You do not know anything. You only know the surface of love."

nā so ramaṇ nā hām ramaṇī,
duṅhu mana manobhav peṣhala jāni

> "He is not the Lover, nor I the Beloved. Both of Our hearts are One." (*Chaitanya Charitamrit* 2.8.194)

For this reason, this love is the innermost experience. If a devotee experiences his Beloved, then his Lord is the Enjoyer and the devotee is the one being enjoyed, and the pleasure experienced by his Lover is the innermost experience for the devotee: in other words, the internal bliss felt by the devotee when his service fills his Lord with joy. In his poetry, the great devotee Rasakhan reflects the essence of this aphorism:

binu jovan gun rūp dhan, binu svārath hit jāni
suddh kāmanā te rahit, prem sakal rasakhāni
ati sūćham komal atihi, ati pataro ati dūr
prem kaṭhin sab te sadā nit ikras bharpūr
rasamay svābhāvik vinā svārath achal mahān
sadā ekras baṛat nit suddh prem rasakhān

> "That love which cares not for looks, money or age, which is pure and beyond the touch of selfish wanting, is a treasure-trove of pure sweetness. It is exceedingly subtle and tender, very delicate and very distant. It is also the most difficult of all, overflowing with eternal and unchanging ecstasy. That sacred love is naturally delectable, selfless, unwavering, always rapturous and ever-increasing - so says the poet Rasakhan."

Sutra 55

|| *tat prāpya tadevāvalokayati tadeva śr̥ṇoti tadeva bhāṣayati tadeva cintayati* ||

After the attainment of sacred love, the devotee sees nothing but love, hears only about love, speaks only of love and thinks only of love.

Here, Sage Narad describes how the nature of a devotee blossoms when he is in a loving relationship with the Lord. As a lover, he sees his Beloved everywhere and in everything. He thinks about and only sees His Love. Even with the external worldly distractions, his mind is constantly meditating on his Lord and relentlessly remembering Him. The devotee fails to see and enjoy objects disconnected from his Beloved.

A *gopi* once said:

jit dekhauň tit syāmamaī hai
syām kuñj ban jamunā syāmā, syām gagan ghan ghaṭā ćhaī hai
sab raṅganmeň syām bharo hai, log kahat yaha bāt naī hai
maiň baurī kī loganhīkī syām putariyā badal gaī hai
chandrasār ravisār syām hai mr̥gamad syām kām bijaī hai
nīlkanṭhko kanṭh syām hai mano syāmatā bel baī hai
śrutiko aćchar syām dekhiyat dīpsikhāpar syāmataī hai
nar devankī kaun kathā hai alakh brahm ćhabi syāmamaī hai

> "Everything I see is saturated with Shyam. The bower is *shyam*,[54] the cloudy sky is *shyam*, the Yamuna River is *shyam*. All the colours are imbued with *shyam*. People are telling me this is something strange! Have I gone insane, or have the pupils in everyone's eyes become *shyam*? The sun and moon are *shyam*, all the musk is permeated with *shyam*. Lord Shiv's throat is *shyam* [from swallowing the poison after the churning of the milk ocean]. The vine of love growing in my heart is *shyam*. The letters of the scriptures are definitely *shyam* and the wick of the candle is also *shyam*. What to speak of men and gods, even the formless Absolute looks like *shyam* to me!" (*Vrajwasi Poetry*)

---

[54] This poem is a play on words. The word *shyam* can mean dark or more specifically, lovely and black with a bluish tinge. Shyam is also one of Krishn's most prominent Names.

The poet Thakur captures the very essence of a devotee in this state:

kānan dūsro nām sunai nahi ekahi rańg rańgo yaha ḍoro
dhokhehu dūsro nām kaṛhai rasanā mukh bāńdhi halāhal boro
ṭhākur chittakī vṛtti yahai ham kaisehu ṭek tajaiń nahi bhoro
bāvarī ve ańkhiyāń jari jāyń jo sāvaro ćhaańḍi nihārati goro

> "Our ears refuse to hear any name but His, for the thread of our fate is dyed in Shyam's colour alone. If we were to say any other name, it would be like pouring poison on our tongues and binding our mouths shut. The poet Thakur says, 'Our hearts and our entire minds, even the subconscious mind, are so overtaken by Him, we can never, even unconsciously, act otherwise. If our crazy eyes try to give up Shyam to behold any other colour, burn them and let us go blind.'"

In this state of being, every sound that permeates the lover's ear is nothing but the sweetest melody of his Beloved's love-song. He never tires of praising Him because in every word that he speaks, he enjoys the incomparable flavour of the nectar of sacred love. All the limbs of his body feel only the presence of his Beloved. The lover's heart is unable and unwilling to expand for anyone else. His love transforms into the reflection of his Beloved.

Drowning in the ocean of love is an indescribable feeling, and it is the highest state of infinite bliss. Hence, the *Chandogya Upanishad* (7.24.1) mentions, "The state of the Infinite is the state in which nothing else is seen, nor heard, nor thought of. That which is Infinite is immortal and that which is finite is mortal." This is sacred love. It is whole and it intensifies with each passing moment. The flow is unbroken, subtler than the subtlest, and therefore, it cannot be defined.

Sutra 56

|| *gauṇī tridhā guṇabhedādārtādibhedād vā* ||

There are three kinds of secondary devotion mentioned according to the nature of the devotee.

Thus far, the topmost superior type of devotion has been discussed: one in which the loving devotee attains his beloved Lord in the form of sacred love. In this aphorism, Sage Narad describes the secondary type of devotion, of a lower order, which has three types of qualities: *sattva*, *rajas* and *tamas*, also associated with the three types of spiritual aspirants: the seeker of truth, the seeker of worldly gain and the distressed.

Secondary devotion can be defined in conjunction with the three qualities as follows:

- *Sattva*: "Devotion that is performed in the form of relinquishing the results of one's actions as an offering to the Lord with the intention of eliminating sins, or in which worship is performed as a matter of duty, with the understanding that one is the servant of the Lord, is *sattvik* devotion." (*Srimad Bhagwatam* 3.29.10)

- *Rajas*: "Devotion that is motivated by desire for material gain, power and fame and is practiced solely through the form of image worship is *rajasik* devotion." (*Srimad Bhagwatam* 3.29.9)

- *Tamas*: "Devotion catalysed by anger, hypocrisy, jealousy or violence is *tamasik* devotion." (*Srimad Bhagwatam* 3.29.8)

The seeker of truth (the *sattvik* devotee), the seeker of worldly wealth (the *rajasik* devotee) and the distressed (the *tamasik* devotee) practice three different types of devotion, therefore secondary devotion is divided into three categories, according to the different aspirations of the devotee.

The *Bhagwad Gita* mentions four types of devotees:

(i) The knowledgeable: The knowledgeable devotee is one who is disinterested with the material world, who has realised the Lord and who sees only Him as the permanent reality. There is nothing other than the Lord Himself. He practices devotion under the natural inclination of his heart. This aphorism is not talking about this type of devotee.

(ii) The distressed: A distressed devotee is one who is *tamasik*. He tries to make offerings to please Krishn because he wants to defeat his enemy or his competitor. Demons are *tamasik*. There is a mountain on the bank of the Gandaki River in Nepal, where a demon meditated to please Lord Krishn, in order to receive a boon. When the Lord was pleased by the demon's devotion, He Himself came to bestow a fruit for the austerity. The demon had meditated for many years whilst fasting, and when he received an audience with Lord Krishn, the demon failed to realise that the Lord was the object of his meditation and austerity for many years. The sight of Lord Krishn's soft and beautiful body made the demon hungry and he asked the Lord if he could eat Him. The demon tried to attack Krishn but he was unsuccessful in his attempt. The merciful Krishn fulfilled his desire and made him an insect which eats *shaligram shila* (the black stone form of Krishn).

The characteristics of one who is affected by *tamas* are lethargy and anger. Yet devotional practice can even offer opportunities for the *tamasik* devotees to perform devotion according to their nature. For example, if an aspirant is going to sleep, he can imagine resting his head at the lotus feet of Lord Krishn, taking His shelter. Upon waking, the aspirant may reminisce about how he spent the whole night under the shelter of the Lord of his heart, bowing at His feet.

(iii) The seeker of worldly wealth: This is a *rajasik* devotee. In the *Srimad Bhagwatam*, Prince Dhruv had the grand desire to be king of the three Universes. Through intense devotional practice, he tried to please Krishn, with the hope that the Lord would fulfil his desire. When Krishn appeared before Dhruv, to reward him a boon, his worldly desire vanished and instead, Dhruv asked for the benediction of eternal service to the Lord. The *Bhaktirasamrtasindhu* mentions two types of devotees: the desiring and the desireless. By making one's desires limited, once those desires are fulfilled, one becomes a desireless devotee. Thus, it is essential for the *rajasik* devotee that he conditions himself to limit his desires.

(iv) The seeker of truth: This is a devotee who is inquisitive and *sattvik*. Once, the Sanat Kumars went to the Lord's abode. They paid obeisances to Him. By bowing down at the lotus feet of the Lord, the fragrance of *Tulsi*[55] suffused their senses. The Sanat Kumars went into a trance, experiencing the beauty of *Tulsi*. Thereafter, they started performing devotion because they had the urge to experience the source of *Tulsi*'s happiness, which they could only imagine to be the most beautiful feeling. By this offering, they merited the gift of an audience with *Tulsi*'s love, Lord Krishn Himself.

Hence, there are four types of devotees: the knowledgeable, the distressed, the seeker of worldly wealth and the seeker of truth. The practice of this secondary type of devotion is not directly beneficial because it is not a direct path to attain sacred love, even though it is righteous. By practicing this kind of devotion, the devotees attain the mercy of the Lord, which leads them to the highest stage on their spiritual path, in other words, primary devotion or devotion in the form of sacred love. Each person has some combination of *sattva, rajas and tamas* in them. Of these three qualities, the prevalence of one above the other two determines the nature of the aspirant. Nevertheless, each category guides one towards pure devotion because every kind of devotional practice contains a constituent of the following elements: remembrance of the Lord, contemplation on the Lord and dependence on the Lord. Therefore, any form of devotion is never in vain and one should always make a point of practicing devotion in whatever form it is accessible.

---

[55] *Tulsi* is a plant commonly known as Holy Basil, and in Lord Vishnu's abode (*Vaikunth*), she is one of His wives. The scriptures mention that Lord Krishn accepts offerings made with the leaf of a *tulsi* plant.

Sutra 57

|| *uttarasmāduttarastmātpūrvapūrvā śreyāya bhavati* ||

Among these, each preceding category is superior to the succeeding one.

Rajasik is better than *tamasik* and *sattvik* is better than *rajasik*. Similarly, the devotional practice by the seeker of truth is purer than that of the seeker of worldly wealth and the devotional practice of the seeker of worldly wealth is more refined than that of the distressed.

Sutra 58

|| *anyasmāt saulabhyaṁ bhaktau* ||

The Lord is easier to attain by devotion than by any other path.

In Ayurved (traditional holistic Indian medicine) there are three types of medicine: medicine made from bark, medicine made from ashes and medicine made from the essence of various leaves and flowers. The path of knowledge and renunciation is like medicine made from bark; it is bitter, not suitable for everyone and very few patients can consume it. In the same manner, one needs a lot of patience, discipline and renunciation to follow this path. On the path of knowledge, a person has to constantly debate and his success depends on the strength of his argument. Yet there is always a doubt in the ability of his knowledge to steer him in the direction of the Lord.

The medicine made from ashes is like the path of action, and to follow this path one needs to be disciplined whilst performing any ritualistic ceremony for the Lord. Inconsistencies in the scriptural procedures can have a negative impact on the devotee. One also needs to fulfil all of the requirements of the procedure for the rituals according to the scriptures, and this becomes a costly process (the medicine made of ashes is expensive); therefore, not everyone is eligible to tread this path. If a doctor advises a poor patient to take expensive medication daily and frequently, it would not be feasible for him to do so. On the path of action, one can attain certain objects but once again, the certainty of receiving the fruits of one's actions remains in doubt.

The medicine made from essences (*rasayan*) is like the path of devotion; thus, it is for everyone. Scholars have stated that the path of devotion is like vital medicine because anyone can consume it and anyone can cure himself with it. This essential medicine is Krishn Himself. This path does not require one to be a scholar of the scriptures, wealthy, from a privileged position in a good family or in society, austere, wise, dispassionate, and so forth.

One only needs childlike faith in Him and constant remembrance of Him. When these two elements are there, devotion starts to manifest itself. The *Bhagwad Gita* (9.30) states, "If someone worships Me single-mindedly, even if he commits sins, he should be considered a divine person for the sake of that sacred commitment."

On the path of devotion there is not the slightest doubt of an aspirant pleasing Lord Krishn. It is mentioned in the *Gautamiya Tantra*: "Sri Krishn is so loving towards His devotees that He sells Himself to any one of them who offers Him a *tulsi* leaf and a palmful of water."

On this path there are no restrictions on loving the Lord and how one should love Him. Any aspirant can choose any kind of service to please Him. The devotee Shabri had taken the service of cleaning a path used by spiritual personalities to go to the river. She would clean before sunrise so that no one would get hurt from the stones and the thorns. And when those spiritual personalities would bathe in the river, she used to silently enter their *ashram*[56] to clean it. When Lord Krishn incarnated as Lord Ram, He did not go to the spiritual personalities who worshipped Him ritualistically for thousands of years. Instead, Lord Ram gave Shabri an audience with Him, purely because she was following the path of devotion.

In the subsequent story, the Lord also enjoys the love of Vidur, the son of a maidservant, who was deeply devoted to Him. One day, to prevent a war between the Pandavs and the Kauravs, Lord Krishn came as an ambassador for the Pandavs, to ask the Kauravs if a compromise could be reached. The idea was firmly rejected and the Kauravs invited the Lord to eat at their palace. But Krishn declined their proposal because they were not devotees. Instead, He went to the home of His great devotee Vidur, who was not present at the time. Vidur's wife was overwhelmed by seeing Krishn and whilst staring at Him, she started to peel a banana for Him. Completely mesmerised, she threw away the banana and offered Him the peel, which He ate without hesitation.

The moment Vidur arrived home, he found that the bananas were uneaten and Lord Krishn was consuming the peels. When Vidur questioned his wife's behaviour, she immediately realised her mistake and started offering the bananas. Thereafter, Lord Krishn explained that the banana peels tasted far sweeter than the bananas themselves. This is the nature of Krishn; He was relishing the object that was offered to Him with loving devotion.

---

[56] An *ashram* is a solitary place of living with the most basic facilities, particularly suitable for austere aspirants who want to focus on their spiritual practice.

A wife turns only to her husband for her support, and their child grabs his father's finger when he wants to walk, because both are reassured that as a father and a husband, the man will always be there for them. This is love and this is faith. Similarly, on the path of devotion, Lord Krishn Himself comes to guide and nourish those devotees who seek Him with complete faith and love.

Sutra 59

|| *pramāṇāntarasyānapekṣatvāt svayaṁ pramāṇatvāt* ||

Devotion does not depend upon any other proof because it is itself the proof.

When an aspirant treads the path of action, he invokes the Lord to witness his action, to judge whether the act is performed correctly, and then the Lord rewards the fruits of that deed. On the contrary, the path of devotion does not require any proof. Here, the analogy of a courthouse can be used. When an offender appears in front of the presiding judge, the court asks for witnessess to determine whether the offender's actions were right or wrong (the path of action). On the path of devotion, the Lord is the judge and the witness Himself, and when He has already experienced sacred love from His ardent devotee, the Lord has no need to seek any other proof, because this love is conclusive evidence.

The path of action requires one to perform and engage in activities related to the external world, but the path of devotion is an inner journey of personal exploration because it is a trail that begins within the heart of the lover. It is more of an internal process of feelings and one should not display those innermost sentiments to the rest of the world, just as a lover would not betray his intimacy to anyone else. This inner sanctity is where the Lord of one's heart resides. For this reason, aspirants should not question each other's devotion because devotion is an internal process of the heart which requires no proof or evidence. The devotee needs enough personal confidence and conviction to believe that he is devotional. It is possible for an aspirant to be delusional about his journey on the path of devotion, but it is important to note that delusion is not a permanent state of being. For example, in the dark, a rope may appear to be a snake, yet simply by lighting a candle, one can see the reality. In the same manner, if the fire of devotion burns steadily then self-delusion is just an illusion, which vanishes by the mercy of Lord Krishn's love.

Sutra 60

|| *śāntirūpātparamānandarūpācca* ||

The path of devotion is easier than other paths because its nature is of supreme peace and supreme bliss.

When the heart is completely satisfied, it is in a state of peace and supreme bliss. Until one experiences fulfilment in one's heart, one remains restless. Material happiness or desires no longer affect an aspirant who feels and sees supreme bliss in the form of Lord Krishn in his heart. A devotee who has attained devotion sees Radha and Krishn in beautiful Vrindavan within his heart, accompanied by Their cows and companions. Here, he witnesses the Divine Couple's play with each other and this state gives unlimited peace and supreme bliss to the devotee's heart.

8

Precautions

Sutra 61

|| *lokahānau cintā na kāryā niveditātmalokavedatvāt* ||

The devotee should not worry about worldly losses because he has surrendered himself and his temporal and spiritual interests to the Lord.

The *Hari Bhakti Vilas* (11.417) elaborates on the process of surrendering:

> The six aspects of full surrender are: (1) accepting things favourable for devotion, (2) rejecting things unfavourable for devotion, (3) believing firmly in the Lord's protection, (4) feeling exclusively dependent on the mercy of the Lord for one's maintenance, (5) having no interest separate from the Lord, and (6) always feeling meek and humble before the Lord, with complete surrender to Him.

Surrendering to the Lord means to offer to Him everything that one possesses. The *Bhakti Sandarbh* classifies this process into two types: ordinary and extraordinary. Ordinary surrender is associated with an aspirant who is lacking a stable taste for devotion and extraordinary surrender is associated with an aspirant who is permeated with intense devotional nectar. The *Bhakti Sandarbh* (section 309) states, "There are two types of self-surrender: that which is inspired by a particular type of loving feelings, and that which is not." In the first type of self-surrender, one gives up the attachments to wealth (*arth*), physical or emotional pleasure (*kaam*) and religious duties (*dharm*). These offerings are made as matter of obligation, and they are made without loving feelings:

> Scripture mentions three goals of human life: *kaam*, *arth* and *dharm*. Within the pursuit of these three fall law, education, self-realisation, *Vedic* ritual, logic and all the methods of earning one's livelihood. All of these are peripheral or

> external subjects of the ancient scriptures and are thus material. But surrender to the lotus feet of the Lord is the essence of the scriptures. (*Srimad Bhagwatam* 7.6.26)

In the second type of self-surrender, the offering is made when one is fully absorbed in love for the Lord. In a love letter to Krishn, Rukmini, who became one of His wives, wrote the following words: "My Lord, I therefore choose You as my Husband, and I offer myself unto You as Your wife. O Beloved with the lotus-petal eyes! Please come and take me without delay, lest Shishupal snatch what is rightfully Yours, like a jackal stealing the lion's prize." (*Srimad Bhagwatam* 10.52.39)

Surrender should not be misinterpreted as defeat because defeat readily implies weakness or failure. Sage Narad is not discussing the nature of one who quits at the first sign of difficulty. He is illustrating the nature of one who is independent and able to give up whatever is necessary for the sake of devotion. And by this practice, the devotee ceases to be a slave to his own ego and becomes the Lord's entirely. Here, there is no question of loss for the devotee because whatever belongs to the Lord extends to those who surrender to Him. "Just as one does not worry about livestock once it has been sold to another, so a person who has offered his body to the Lord need no longer worry about his own wellbeing." (*Bhaktirasamrtasindhu* 1.2.197)

Therefore, belonging to the Lord of his heart, the one who has surrendered grieves not for worldly losses.

Sutra 62

|| na tatsiddhau lokavyavahāro heyaḥ kintu phalatyāgastatsādhanaṁ ca kāryameva ||

Until one has attained devotion, one should not discard the good worldly activities. But devotion should be practiced renouncing the fruit of those activities.

Here, Sage Narad advises the aspirant not to deliberately abandon the good worldly activities. The assumption that a devotee develops a cold heart and becomes a recluse because of his one-pointedness for the Lord is unfounded. When sacred love is realised, worldly and religious activities automatically fade away. One who only practices renouncing the fruits of his action carries out his duties in a neutral way, and he automatically becomes free from the worries of tension and loss.

This type of devotee is mentioned in the following story. A spiritual master named Samarth Swami Sri Ram Das was travelling across a forest with his disciples. In the heat of the afternoon, they took shelter of a tree, near a big well. A branch from one of the trees was hanging over the well. Sri Ram Das asked his disciple Amba Das if he could climb the tree and cut the branch in order to prevent the dry leaves from falling into the well and making the water dirty. All of the other disciples, who were audience to the conversation between the two, began to feel anxious because there was no supportive branch from which to cut the overhanging branch and there was danger of falling into the well. The disciples tried to prevent Amba Das from carrying out the fatal instruction, but there was no use because for Amba Das, his spiritual master's order was of the utmost importance.

Just as he was about to proceed, his spiritual master said, "Oh fool! You will fall into the well if you cut the branch!"

"When your blessings can save me from the ocean of illusion, then what to speak of this small well?" Amba Das replied.

His spiritual master said, "If your faith is such, then continue."

Amba Das started cutting and eventually he fell into the well. All the disciples watched in fear, but Sri Ram Das was sitting very peacefully and chanting. They ran to the edge of the well to search for Amba Das and to their astonishment, they saw the Lord rescuing Amba Das and he emerged from the well without injury.

Thus, one should not worry about the lack or loss of appreciation from others while practicing the path of devotion. Faith in the Lord is a very important aspect of devotion. Often, people who lack self-confidence and faith in their personal actions and goals walk away when others criticize them, for example in a work environment. A devotee is not affected in the same way, for he declares to the Lord, "I am Yours." Becoming a servant of the Lord, the devotee does not leave Him for the sake of his material interests. In the *Advaita-siddhi*, Madhusudhan Saraswati wrote, "You can praise or criticize the author of this book. I have no feeling of being the author, so how does your praise or criticism concern me?" The work that a devotee performs, he does for the pleasure of Krishn, and he offers all his work, not to make others happy or to impress them, but to make his Lord happy.

Sutra 63

|| *strīdhananāstika caritraṁ na sravaṇīyam* ||

Talks about women (sex), wealth, non-believers and enemies are not to be heard.

"Desire, anger and greed are three gateways to agony. They bring about one's destruction. One should give them up." (*Bhagwad Gita* 16.21)

This *Bhagwad Gita* verse nicely elaborates on aphorism 63. But herein, Sage Narad will clarify the point he makes in this aphorism and the point he made in the preceding ones. Previously, Sage Narad asked devotees to be involved in worldly activities, but here he advises what should not be enjoyed for the sake of worldly affairs.

The first point is, "Talks about women (sex) . . . are not to be heard." Narad is not saying to avoid the association of women; he is asking devotees to stay away from the company of women associated with lust. Sage Narad is informing spiritual aspirants to steer clear of three things, namely lust, anger and greed, mentioned in the *Bhagwad Gita* (16.21). Thus, for men, lusty talks about women are to be strictly avoided and for women, lusty talks about men are to be shunned. Avoiding women who are devotees is not possible nor is it mentioned in this aphorism, even though many spiritual masters have commentated that this aphorism instructs devotees to cut contact with all women.

From the beginning, the *Narad Bhakti Sutra* clearly states that devotion is for everyone, therefore it would make no sense for Narad to discriminate against women. Sage Narad himself described devotion using the example of the *gopis*, the most elevated devotees. And there are countless examples of great inspirational women devotees who revolutionised devotion and paved the way for the rest of the spiritual world to follow - women such as Mirabai, Shabri, Karmaitri Bai, Silpillai, Kunti, Devahuti, Vrinda, and so forth. Hence, the essence of this aphorism states that one whose mind is engrossed in lusty thoughts or attracted towards men or women can never contemplate single-mindedly on the Lord because lust gives rise to passion and becomes a blockage in devotion.

The second part of the aphorism mentions wealth, which refers to greed here. When feelings of greed arise, an aspirant loses his sense of judgement regarding what is good and bad. He creates his own definition of devotion according to his whims. This self-indulgence only makes him meditate about his object of desire and becomes an obstruction in devotional life.

The last point of the aphorism guides devotees to remove themselves from situations where they hear about atheists and enemies, which can lead to feelings of anger. One can boldly say that in the world no one is an atheist because to prove the hypothesis of whether the Lord exists or not, one has to sincerely perform devotional practice. If the scriptures state that one who treads this path will attain the Lord, the atheist has to practice these instructions and test for himself whether they are true or not before drawing an affirmative conclusion; an atheist has performed no such practice. In this aphorism, an atheist is referred to as a *nastik*, which means incomplete in Sanskrit. A person who is incomplete, with no yearning to find the means to complete himself, will only speak about subject matter that is not whole. Atheists will only speak negatively about spirituality, the Lord, the spiritual master, and the rituals described in the scriptures. Of the two senses, sound has a deeper impact on a person than sight. The heart is the house of the soul as well as the Supreme Soul. A devotee should not allow dirt to enter and settle in his heart by hearing any profanity regarding spiritual life, the spiritual master, the Lord and the practice which he performs.

In summary, talks about lusty people, wealth, atheists and enemies are not to be heard. "By paying attention to the things which attract the senses, one becomes attached to those things. From attachment, desire comes and from desire comes anger." (*Bhagwad Gita* 2.62)

Sutra 64

|| *abhimānadambhādikaṁ tyājyam* ||

Pride, pretence and other vices should be abandoned.

"Oh Lord! Those who are proud of their social status, power, wealth and education become incapable of taking Your Name. But You grant Your direct personal audience to humble people." (*Srimad Bhagwatam* 1.8.26)

The preceding aphorism discussed certain abstentions a devotee should adhere to, namely, he should not participate in conversation about wealth, non-believers or enemies, or that which stimulates lust. This aphorism adds to its predecessor and warns that if a devotee feels he has overcome these obstacles, this attitude may also cultivate a sense of pride in him. A proud person may think that there is no one better than him. Often, on the path of knowledge an aspirant thinks that he is *Brahman* (The Absolute).

Whether or not the person becomes *Brahman* is not the point. The point is that by identifying himself as *Brahman*, he starts to believe he is the Lord and becomes proud. When an aspirant performs any ritual on the path of action, he offers the ritual to the Lord in return for the fruits of his deed, which can come from a worldly desire. Therefore, this path of action can also provoke pride in the aspirant, making him believe that he is the doer. The feeling of pride in the performance of austerities or believing oneself to be the controller can also arise in one who follows the path of disciplined contemplation. These kinds of pride can spiral into other prides, where the aspirant starts to think that he is the doer in his spiritual practice; for example, the temple was built by him, he fed hundreds of devotees regularly, he performed many rituals, and so forth. But on the path of devotion, pride will divert one away from attaining the goal.

The *Bhagwad Gita* (18.61) states, "The Lord resides in the hearts of all beings, piloting the vehicle in which they have become passengers by the influence of *maya* (illusion)." Therefore, if the Lord is the guiding force and the devotee is His instrument, then the devotee cannot be the doer. "I know the difference between right and wrong, but I cannot get myself to do right – I cannot stop myself from doing wrong. O Master of the Senses! You dwell in my heart and I will do as You would have me do." (*Mahabharat*)

On the path of devotion, one becomes the servant of the Lord. In this role, whatever works the aspirant performs, he executes for Krishn alone; therefore the aspirant develops no pride. "You are my real Mother and Father, my true Friend and my Family. You are my Wisdom and my Wealth. You are Everything to me, O Lord of Lords." (*Prapanna Gita*, verse 28)

In the *Bhagwad Gita* (16.4), Lord Krishn speaks about pretence, and He states that this characteristic is very dangerous for any devotee. If someone has greed, lust or anger, he is aware that he has these qualities and others can also find such defects in him. But pretence is a characteristic which is generally not acceptable in a person, and eventually pretentious persons may even forget that they are pretending. Their artificial reality becomes a reality for them. For example, whilst chanting an aspirant suddenly changes his behaviour simply because someone walks by. The aspirant sits attentively, closes his eyes, straightens his posture and starts to chant with full vigour, when he is fully aware that this is not part of his daily devotional practice and he is merely showing off. This illustrates a symptom of pretence. On the path of devotion, the less serious devotees pretend that they are elevated souls by exhibiting a false outer appearance and showing themselves to be something which they are not. In this aphorism, Sage Narad strongly recommends abstention from pride, pretence and other such vices for those who sincerely want to attain devotion.

Sutra 65

|| *tadarpitākhilācāraḥ san kāmakrodhābhimānādikaṁ tasminneva karaṇīyam* ||

One should devote all actions to the Lord and direct one's desire, anger, pride, and so forth, towards Him.

Sage Narad advises the aspirant who has offered all actions to the Lord to also utilise desire, anger and pride in His service. In the *Prem Bhakti Chandrika*, Narottam Das Thakur says the same:

> I will put lust, anger, greed, illusion, envy and pride to work, each in its own way. Thus, I can defeat these enemies with a blissful heart and easily worship Krishn. I offer my lust to the service of Krishn, my anger towards the enemies of His devotees and my greed towards association with saints and topics of Krishn. I am deluded without my beloved Lord, and I am proud when I sing His glories. Thus, I make these enemies serve my Beloved.

One may question how these negative emotions can be directed towards the Lord. It is important to note that pure devotees are not subject to feelings of lust, anger, and so forth, which ordinarily haunt the material man. The sentiments of worldly desire, anger, and so forth, are described in the previous aphorisms. Pure souls (devotees and saints) do not yearn for self-satisfaction because they have only one desire and this is to make their Beloved happy; therefore, on the path of sacred love, such feelings are not aroused in them. These devotees become indifferent to the material world and its negative emotions and they become divine in character.

ghar tajauň van tajauň nāgar nagar tajauň
baňsīvaṭ taṭ tajauň kāhū pai na lajihauň
deh tajauň geh tajauň neh kahau kaise tajauň
āj rāj kāj sab ese sāj sajihauň
bāvaro bhayo hai lok bāvarī kahat mokauň
bāvarī kahe te maiň kāhu nā barajihauň
kahaiyā sunaiyā tajau bāp aur bhaiyā tajauň
daiya tajau maiyā pai kanhaiyā nāhi tajihauň

> "I would leave my home, renounce my town and townsmen, to the forest bid farewell. I would give up dear Vanshivat[57] [my Beloved's playground], without the slightest hesitation. I would give up my life, I would leave all I have, but how could I give up my loving? The whole world has gone mad, and they call me mad. Let them call me crazy, I will not argue with them. I could stop talking or listening to anyone. I would give up my own father. Oh! I would give up my mother, but I would never give up Kanhaiya."[58] (*Vrajwasi Poetry*)

There is a wonderful play and sweet exchange of sentiments between the Lord and His devotees where even emotions of anger, desire and pride are the glorious rays emanating from sacred love. The yearning of devotees can be expressed using the example of a relationship between a child and his mother. If anyone offers the child candy, chocolate or toys, or promises to give him the moon in exchange for his mother, he will never accept because he has no real knowledge of or desire for anything except for his mother.

In the same way, devotees crave the Lord and nothing else. When a small child tries to walk and falls down, he begins to cry and when his mother hears him, she leaves everything and runs to her child. The child may get frustrated and show anger towards his mother because he feels she is the cause of his suffering. He becomes unresponsive to his mother's affection. The child recognizes his claim over his mother, who is everything to him. If the child is hungry, if he stumbles and falls or if he is unable to sleep, then his mother is at fault and she is punished with anger, and he shows his pride to her. In the same manner, a devotee who is completely dependent on the Lord can make Him the object of his anger, desire and pride.

The following examples are given to illustrate how desire, anger and pride can become a wonderful play and sweet exchange of sentiments between the Lord and His devotees:

1. Desire: A pure devotee only desires to live or die for the sake of his Lord. He even prays that after his death, the five elements of his body should be used in the service of the Lord.

   > Let my body pass away; may the elements therein join with the primordial elements. I bow before

---

[57] Vanshivat is a banyan tree in Vrindavan where Krishn played the flute and called the *gopis* to the *Raas Mandal*.

[58] Kanhaiya is another name for Krishn.

Brahma – the creator – and beg from him this boon: may the water of my body merge with the water of the lake where Krishn bathes. May the fire of my body merge with the light on Krishn's mirror. May the ether of my body become the space in His courtyard. May the earth of my body mingle with the ground on which He walks, and may the air of my body enter the breeze of the fan that cools Him. (*Padyavali*, verse 340)

2. Anger: Once, Radha became angry with Krishn. When Radha's friend came to pacify Her, She became angrier and was unable to contain Her emotion. This exact scene and Radha's expressions are mentioned in a poem from Vraj:

milauň na tin soň bhūl ab jaulauň jīvan jiyauň
sahauň birah ko sūl baru tāki jvālā jarauň
maiň ab apane man yaha ṭhāni un ke paňth piuň nahiň pānī
kabahu nain na aňjan lāuň mṛgamad bhūli na aṅg chaṛhāuň
sunauň na śravanani ali pika bānī nīl jalaj parasau nahiň pānī

"I will never meet with Him again, as long as I live. I would rather live with the spear of estrangement lodged in My heart, burning in the fire of grief. I resolve never to tread the paths where He walks. All dark things I forsake, for He is dark-skinned. Never again shall kohl adorn My eyes, nor musk perfume Me. I close My ears to the black bee and the cuckoo, and renounce My favourite, the blue lotus." (*Vrajwasi Poetry*)

From the poem, one can feel the intensity of Radha's love for Her beloved Krishn even though She is angry at Him. All the scriptures revealed that She was unable to bear any form of separation from Her Beloved, not even for the shortest amount of time measurable. He is the very breath of Her life, yet Radha still exhibits Her anger towards Krishn for the mischievous pranks He plays on Her.

3. Pride: On another occasion, Radha became unhappy with Krishn and adopted a firm attitude towards Him. She told Her friends:

sakhi naňdlāl na āvan pāvai
bhītar charan dharan jin dījo chāhe jite lalchāvaiň

aisan ko bisvās kahā rī kapaṭ bain batirāvaiṅ
nārāyaṇ ik mero bhavan taji anat cahaiṅ jahāṅ jāvai

"My dear friends! Do not let Krishn in. Though He may beg and plead, He must not set foot inside. How can we trust a cheater like Him? May He go wherever He pleases, as long as He does not come here." (*Vrajwasi Poetry*)

This ode, written by a devotee named Narayan, shows a beautiful state of pride. The Lord defeated so many demons effortlessly, but this time He was powerless to reconcile with Radha.

Sutra 66

|| *trirūpabhaṅgapūrvakaṁ nityadāsyanityakāntābhajanātmakaṁ prema kāryaṁ premaiva kāryam* ||

Rising above the three categories of devotion (mentioned in aphorism 56), sacred love and sacred love alone should be cultivated in the mood of constant service to the Lord, either as a devoted servant or wife.

In this aphorism, Sage Narad says that once the aspirant goes beyond the three qualities of material nature – *tamas*, *rajas* and *sattva* – he should serve the Lord with sacred love. The following example illustrates how one should serve with love for the sake of pure service. A spiritual master asked one of his disciples, who was serving him food, to fetch some water. Another disciple was allocated water service, but he was absent at the time. So, the disciple who was serving the food replied that he was unable to serve water as he was not given this service. Sage Narad stresses that the nature of the service is not as important as the inclination to serve the spiritual master or the Lord, which is essential. Therefore, this aphorism advises the devotee to act like a good servant or a good wife, whose service is unwavering and constant. A good servant serves his master in this manner and the same can be said about the service of a good wife towards her husband. However, the aspirant should serve the Lord with tender love regardless of His form. Usually, people fight because they have an affinity for a particular form of the Lord and they refuse to serve any of His other forms, whether it is Lord Krishn, Jesus Christ, Allah, Lord Ram, Lord Shiv, and so forth.

The *Bhakti Sandarbh* (section 106) reveals a story, from the *Vishnu Dharmottar Puran,* of a landlord who was a devotee of Shiv. When the landlord became sick, he asked his son to call a priest to perform worship on his behalf. So his son asked a priest, a follower of Lord Narsingh, to come and perform worship of Shiv. The priest refused, making the son angry. The landlord's son threatened to kill the priest and out of fear, he agreed to perform the worship. A fond lover of Lord Narsingh, the priest contemplated on how he would venerate Shiv, who is the presiding lord of ignorance (*tamas*) when Lord Narsingh is the Slayer of ignorance. The priest felt that if he worshipped the god of ignorance, he might become ignorant himself. He felt that if he were to take Shiv as Narsingh and worship Him, only then would he attain a positive result and the ignorance, which may manifest in him, would vanish. The priest proceeded with the worship of Shiv by chanting hymns to Lord Narsingh. Overhearing this, the landlord's son was filled with rage. He armed himself with a sword and charged towards the priest. At the same time, Lord Narsingh manifested from the Shiv deity and killed the landlord's son. Here, the devotee is not betraying the Lord because he realises the fundamental point: that the Lord is omnipotent and omnipresent. Thus, a lover sees his Lord in all His forms and in all of His creation.

Once, when a devotee named Bilvamangal Thakur went to Ayodhya,[59] a sage teased him by saying, "Your Lord (Krishn) has a flute and a peacock feather crown, and He is a Cowherd Boy from Vrindavan. So have you taken shelter of the King of Ayodhya, Ram, and left that Cowherd Boy?"

Bilvamangal Thakur said, "O Lord Ram, Beloved of Sita, please put aside Your bow and arrows for a while; take up the flute and wear the peacock feather crown. Then I will bow before You." (*Krishn Karnamrit* 3.94)

Suddenly, in front of everyone, Lord Ram put down His bow and arrows and gave Bilvamangal Thakur a vision of Himself as Lord Krishn.

Saint Mirabai worshipped Lord Krishn as her Husband from childhood. In her youth, Mirabai's family married her to King Kumbhrana, yet she continued her devotion as a wife to her beloved Lord. Once, her husband Kumbhrana became angry over an incident involving Mirabai, which he felt brought disgrace to the family honour. He told her to drown herself in the river, and Mirabai obeyed his wishes. As she prepared to step into the waters, a hand from behind grabbed her shoulder and embraced her lovingly. Mirabai turned around and saw her Beloved, Krishn, standing before her. The Lord smiled and whispered softly, "Your life with your material relations is no more now. Rejoice! You are and have always been My dear wife."

mere to girdhar gopāl dūsro na koī
jāke sar mor mukuṭ mero pati soī
tāt māt bhrāt bandhu āpano na koī
ćhāňḍi daī kul ki kāni kahā karihai koī
saňtan ḍhiňg baiṭhi baiṭhi lok lāj khoī

---

[59] Ayodhya is a city in Uttar Pradesh (India) and it was the birthplace of Lord Ram.

chunari ke kiye ṭuk oḍh linhī loī
motī muṅge utār banamālā poī
aṅsuvan jal sīṅchi sīṅchi prem beli boī
ab to bel phail gaī ānaṅd phal hoī
dūdh kī mathaniyā baḍe prem se bilāī
mākhan jab kāṛhi liyo chāćh piye koi
āī maiṅ bhakati kāj jagat dekhi roī
dāsī mīrā lāl giridhar tāro ab mohī
mere to giridhar gopāl dūsro na koī

"Only Krishn is mine, no one else. He who wears the peacock-feather crown is indeed my Husband. My father, my mother, my brother and other relatives are not my own. I have renounced reputation and family honour. What can anyone do to me? I cast away my shyness and family rules to sit in the company of saints. I tore my veil in half and clothed myself in a mendicant's shawl. I took off my pearls and finery and put on a garland of wildflowers. The tears from my eyes watered the vine of sacred love. Now that vine has matured and borne the fruit of bliss. When someone has so lovingly churned the milk and given me butter, why should I forsake it to drink buttermilk? I came here for devotion's sake, but I wept to see the world. Please save me now, for I am Your maidservant. Only You are mine, no one else." (*Mirabai*)

The Lord depends on love alone. Therefore, Sage Narad tells the aspirant not to demand anything from the Lord in exchange for the service rendered unto Him. One can win Lord Krishn either by loving Him as a servant or as a wife.

9

Qualities of the Sacred Lover

Sutra 67

|| *bhaktā ekāntino mukhyāḥ* ||

Devotees who are exclusively attached to the Lord with one-pointedness are the finest.

If a person makes his heart a home and accommodates many relationships and attachments there, he is unable to provide a place of rest for any important and unexpected guests. Any eminent visitor would expect that his every need be taken care of by his host. Suppose the Lord wants to make the devotee's heart His abode and finds there is no room for Him, and the other occupants are not willing to make any adjustments for Him. The Lord will not be served exclusively, nor will He be able to taste the nectar of the devotee's love for Him. Here, Sage Narad speaks of one-pointedness for the Lord, without any other distractions. Being a part of the Lord, a devotee should offer himself to Krishn and whatever duties the devotee performs, he should do so for the Lord only. The devotee should not consider himself separate from the Lord and he should act according to the will of his Master. "He who remembers Me constantly and single-mindedly attains Me easily." (*Bhagwad Gita* 8.14)

One can illustrate this mood beautifully with the story of a sage travelling on a boat full of passengers. Suddenly, whilst crossing the river, the boat started to sink. Water started to flood in from a hole at the bottom of the vessel. In a panic, all of the passengers started to bail the water out as fast as they could, and to their surprise, the sage, who was sitting, rose and started to pour water back into the boat. In the midst of this calamity, the boat somehow began to drift towards the riverbank. So the sage started to pour the water out of the boat and back into the river. Witnessing this odd behaviour from the sage, the passengers became very confused and they questioned his actions. At first, they had accused the sage of trying to kill them by making the boat sink quicker, but then he appeared to save them by bailing the water out of the boat. The sage replied that when the boat started to sink in the middle of the river, he felt it was a call from Lord Krishn and He wanted to take all of them back to His abode. The sage acted according to the will of his Lord, and proceeded to help Him by pouring the water back in. But as the vessel started to drift near the riverbank, the sage felt that it was not the Lord's wish to end their lives, hence he started to pour the water out of the boat. This tale shows the work of a devout and elevated servant of the Lord, who is willing to serve Him single-mindedly and sincerely, in every possible way.

kabirā kājar rekhahu ab to daī na jāy
nainani pītam rami rahā dūjā kahāń samāy
āṭh pahar chauńsaṭh gharī mere aur na koy
nainā māhi tu basai nīňdahi ṭhaur na hoy

"I tried to line my eyes with kohl, but I cannot anymore. When my eyes are so full of my Beloved, what place is there for anything else? Every moment of every day and night, it's only You. My eyes are so full of You not even sleep can enter them." (*Kabir*)

Sutra 68

|| *kaṇṭhāvarodharomāñcāśrubhiḥ parasparaṁ lapamānāḥ pāvayanti kulāni pṛthivīṁ ca* ||

Conversing with one another in broken words, voices choked with emotion, with bristling of their bodily hairs and tears streaming from their eyes, such fine devotees bless their families and the world also.

When fine devotees, such as the ones described in the preceding aphorism, congregate and glorify their much-adored Lord, they feel supreme bliss, and this heightened emotion emanates from every pore in their body, radiating the spotless lustre of sacred love. The following verse from the *Srimad Bhagwatam* (11.14.24) describes an elevated soul, in a deep trance, exhibiting symptoms of ecstatic love: "At times his voice falters, his heart melts, he weeps, he laughs and laughs. At times he feels ashamed, he sings, he dances. Thus, one who remains connected to Me by his unbroken loving service purifies the entire Universe."

Sutra 69

|| tīrthīkurvanti tīrthāni sukarmīkurvanti karmāṇi sacchāstrīkurvanti śāstrāṇi ||

Such devotees increase the sanctity of holy places, render all actions blessed and make the scriptures more sacred.

Yuddhisthir conveyed the sentiment of this aphorism during his conversation with the great devotee Vidur, "The Lord's dear devotees, like you, are themselves *tirths* (holy lands or crossing-over points between the material and spiritual worlds). They make holy lands even holier, because the Lord Himself resides in their hearts." (*Srimad Bhagwatam* 1.13.10)

According to this aphorism and the abovementioned verse, a devotee's heart transforms into a holy place by the power of devotion. Holy water and holy places are considered to be sacred, and visiting, residing and bathing in such lands cleanses a sinner. But as soon as he comes into contact with negative association, he may commit offences again and resume his former identity as an offender.

The goddess Ganga descended on Earth as a river so that people could bathe in her to purify themselves of sin. Prior to coming, an anxious Ganga asked King Bhagirath how she would wash away the accumulated sins of humanity. King Bhagirath eloquently replied, "Mother Ganga! There are great souls, renounced and steadfast in virtue, who spend their lives saving the people. When such saints bathe in you, they will cleanse you of those sins, for the Lord Himself dwells in their hearts." (*Srimad Bhagwatam* 9.9.6)

There are also instances where devotees have rediscovered holy lands. Whilst returning to his estate from a victorious battle, King Vikramaditya and his army stopped at a place unknown to them. At that time, King Vikramaditya met a sage who told him that this unfamiliar place was Ayodhya, which had been laying in ruins for thousands of years. The sage explained that if the king sat in meditation, he would be able to rediscover and experience all the places of Lord Ram's Ayodhya. The king meditated on the pastimes of Lord Ram and he began to see Ayodhya in its former glory, unveiled before him. Through his devoted contemplation, King Vikramaditya revived the city of Ayodhya and all the pastime places of Lord Ram. Similarly, Chaitanya Mahaprabhu rediscovered

Vrindavan, Radha Kund[60] and Shyam Kund, among other holy places in Vraj.

In the *Srimad Bhagwatam* (4.30.37), Prachetas states, "O Lord! Your dear ones wander this world, purifying even the holy lands (which are already naturally pure). How joyous is the coming of Your devotee for one suffering in fear of this material world." Hence, the pious actions of pure souls revived the holy lands and proved the sanctity of the scriptures - scriptures that hold sacred knowledge for mankind.

---

[60] A *kund* is a sacred pool of holy water.

Sutra 70

|| *tanmayāḥ* ||

For they (the finest devotees) are absorbed in the Lord.

Just as a river merges and becomes one with the ocean, a devotee who has surrendered himself completely at the lotus feet of the Lord becomes one with Him. "The teachings presented here will be experienced as internal revelation when received by those great souls who have great loving devotion for the *Guru* and for the Lord." (*Swetaswatar Upanishad* 6.23)

Sutra 71

|| *modante pitaro nṛtyanti devatāḥ sanāthā ceyaṁ bhūrbhavati* ||

On the advent of a fine devotee, his ancestors rejoice, the gods dance in joy, and Mother Earth finds a protector in him.

The word *pitar* refers to one's living parents as well as one's deceased ancestors. A pure devotee is the pride of his parents as well as his family. The scriptures mention that one's departed ancestors rejoice also. They celebrate the advent of a pure devotee in the family because he can perform rituals that can absolve the results of offences committed by his predecessors. These negative results can prevent liberation for the soul. By pleasing the Lord through the act of good deeds by a pure devotee, his ancestor's soul will be elevated. The Lord said to Prahlad:

> Because of your birth in this dynasty, your wicked father has been cleansed of all sin. What to speak of him, if you had twenty-one generations of ancestors, they would all have been purified as well. Any land where My peaceful, blissfully virtuous, unbiased and loving devotees reside is never bereft of auspiciousness. (*Srimad Bhagwatam* 7.10.18-19)

The increasing number of sinners in the world becomes a concern for the gods and they feel that these wrongdoers will somehow gain control of the heavenly planets too. Therefore, when they find this negativity eradicated by the acts of a sincere devotee, who spreads love among people and instructs them to perform pious work, the gods dance in ecstasy.

Any person who takes a birth acquires three types of debts: debts from ancient sages, ancestors and gods. These debts can be repayed by following a number of rituals, which are revealed by the scriptures. If an aspirant gives up the rituals in favour of pure devotion to the Lord, he can overcome his debts because all the gods, sages and ancestors are a part of Him. "A devotee who forsakes the shelter of prescribed action and takes singular refuge of Krishn, the Nurturer of those who receive His shelter, owes nothing to the gods, the sages, other beings, family, friends, guests, mankind or his ancestors. He is no-one else's servant and is not answerable to anyone else." (*Srimad Bhagwatam* 11.5.41)

When the Lord's beloved devotee takes birth, the world receives a saviour because an elevated soul tries to preserve nature as well as the planet. Through constant loving service, a devotee finds his Lord everywhere and in everything, and as a result, he starts to serve and respect all creation, whilst inspiring the world to do the same.

Sutra 72

|| *nāsti teṣu jātividyārūpakuladhanakriyādi bhedaḥ* ||

Among these primary devotees there is no distinction based upon caste, customs, physical appearance, family, wealth, profession, and the like.

The word *bheda*, at the end of this aphorism, means divide. In Sanskrit *bheda* means *bhittih bhedanat* or that which breaks up. Hence, according to Sage Narad, devotion should not and does not split a community. In devotion, anyone can please the Lord. The *Bharadwaj Parisista* states:

> No particular caste, social class, gender, personality traits, job, time, place or stage of life is a prerequisite for the path of devotion. The Lord should be adored and served daily, according to one's ability, by all, whether they be *Brahmins*, warrior caste, businessmen, public servants or others. One should not consider age, and so forth, when deciding whether or not to offer respects to a *Vaishnav*. On the contrary, one should revere them all, even if they are of low caste.

Thus, even if one is not a scholar from a high social order, one can still become an elevated devotee because devotion is superior to knowledge. And this is one of the main points of the aphorism; there should be no discrimination among devotees. The following poem illustrates this point beautifully:

pothi paṛhi paṛhi jag muā paṇḍit huā na koī
ḍhāī akṣar prem kā paṛhe so paṇḍit hoy

> "The world is studying itself to death, but nobody ever became wise simply by study. The true wise man is one who has studied the two–and-a-half syllables of the word *prem*." (*Kabir*)

The message of this poem is expressed by the tale of two friends who entered a confectionary shop. One bought sweets and immediately started eating them. The other went to the shopkeeper and started enquiring about the varieties of sweets that he sold, what ingredients the sweets contained and the process and time required to make them. As they left the shop, the second friend boasted how he had acquired every piece of information about the sweets, whilst the first friend commented on how busy he was enjoying the taste of each and every sweet. Knowledge of an object can give people information on a surface level about the devotional nectar whereas devotional practice gives the sweetness.

In this aphorism, Sage Narad says that elevated devotees do not see differences among devotees based on caste, customs, physical appearance, family, wealth, profession, and so forth. Sometimes devotees differentiate themselves from others in the devotional community based on variations in their spiritual practice. In *Vaishnavism*, there are different schools of philosophy, and they follow their own rules of caste and have their own customs. If the devotees from these schools develop pride as a result of the differences, they can start to feel superior to others.

Here, it is important to note that devotion and observation of caste rules are two separate things which should not be mixed. One may think that by practicing the rituals of higher castes (*Brahmins*) one can attain devotion, but this is not the case because devotees such as the *gopis*, Prahlad, Dhruv, Vidur, and so forth, were not *Brahmins,* nor were they trying to become *Brahmins*. One only remembers them for their unparalleled devotion to the Lord. The only goal is to become a devotee and devotion is for everyone.

> In every era, many persons whose personalities were *rajasik* (passionate) and *tamasik* (slothful or dark) attained Me by virtue of associating with My devotees. Some such persons were demons, while others were heavenly beings. Birds and beasts attained Me, and among humans, I have been attained by businessmen, simple labourers, women and others. Vritasur, Prahlad, Bali, Banasur, Maya and Vibhishan (born to demon families) attained Me, as did Sugriv, Hanuman, Jambavan, Gajendra, and Jatayu (animals). Tuladhar, Dharma-Vyadha, Kubja, the *gopis* and the wives of the *Brahmins* who were making the sacrificial offerings - all of them attained Me, though they performed no austerities, nor did they study scripture to great lengths or worship the great saints. They attained Me just by associating with Me and My devotees. (*Srimad Bhagwatam* 11.12.3-7)

It is not possible for a person to change his caste and blood lineage in his lifetime. If a high caste devotee does not abide by the rules and regulations of his social order, he should not be judged as a bad devotee because the rules and regulations of devotion are different to those of the caste system. A devotee should not be looked down upon on the grounds of birth, caste, creed, and so forth. He should only be judged by his devotion to the Lord. Therefore in the six *Vaishnav* offences, mentioned in the *Skand Puran*, one offence is to discriminate between devotees on the grounds of caste.

Therefore, Sage Narad stresses that in the practice of devotion, caste, customs, external appearance, birth, wealth, profession, and so forth, are of no real importance; what truly matters is one's devotion for the Lord.

Sutra 73

|| *yatastadīyāḥ* ||

Because they (the perfected saints and devotees) are the Lord's very own.

By the potency of their devotion, all devotees become a part of the Lord's divine nature, which permeates them. Therefore, the appearance and lineage of devotees is irrelevant. These devotees lose all sense of pride and authority. They do not assume a position of superiority amongst the devotee community or even the world because in the eyes of the Lord, everyone is equal.

Sutra 74

|| *vādo nāvalambyaḥ* ||

It is improper for any devotee to enter into controversy.

An aspirant must not enter into arguments. The Sanskrit word *tarkāpratiṣṭhānāt*, from the *Brahma Sutra* (2.1.11), means, "Argument is unstable." In this world of disputes, there are and there always will be people who discuss or argue about religious procedure, the Lord, His devotees and spiritual matters. By having such debates they cannot really understand or learn devotion. The *Katha Upanishad* (1.2.9) states, "The truth cannot be realised by intellectual reasoning." Truth is revealed automatically in the pure heart of a devotee who abides in purity and goodness.

Alternatively, a proverb in Sanskrit states:

vāde vāde jāyate tattvabodhaḥ

"Truth is discovered through argument and reasoning."

The act of engaging in a discussion is not the point of contention here. The nature of reasoning can have either a positive or negative effect. For example, an inquisitive devout aspirant places his arguments before his spiritual master, who in turn dispels the doubts of his disciple and enlightens him with the truth. This kind of reasoning is good. On the contrary, inappropriate reasoning and disagreement brings anger, bitterness, and so forth. Hence, another Sanskrit proverb states:

vāde vāde vardhate vairavahniḥ

"Controversy feeds the fire of animosity."

Spiritual discussions and debates should be held between spiritual masters who correctly uphold knowledge of the truth. They are able to transfer this understanding in the most appropriate manner. Nowadays, some devotees feel that by merely reading a few scriptures, they have mastered the philosophies and they have become scholars. Therefore, these devotees feel qualified to discuss spiritual points with other devotees and give their conclusions from their own understanding, which can be incorrect. These unripe devotees fight over advanced spiritual subjects beyond the understanding of their intelligence. As a result, discussions can transform into arguments, which can have a negative impact on the harmony within the devotional world.

Aspirants who are in the process of their spiritual studies and who are in search of realisations are not eligible to expound conclusions without reaching the highest state of devotion. When an aspirant enters into an argument, he loses the spirit of receptivity. Positive influences can be productive for him only when he is receptive. When a person enters into a discussion, he will have his own viewpoint. If he argues with another to establish that only his opinion is the right one, his mind will be diverted from the true spirit of devotion. With such unhelpful thoughts, the mind fails to receive an influx of inspiration, which it obtains when an individual is receptive. This aphorism advises a sincere devotee not to enter into any argument. When a debate is unavoidable, the devotee should say only what is necessary, without offending the recipient with his words and actions.

Sutra 75

|| *bāhulyāvakāśatvād aniyatatvācca* ||

Because there is scope for many different points and none are definitive.

A scholar may put forth his own point of view and although it may sound definitive, there is always room for further exploration of every idea. Another scholar can always come and offer a counter-statement, which could lead to even deeper discussion of the topic. Thus, the latter half of the aphorism says "and none are definitive." From the beginning of time until the present day, many debates have taken place between scholars, scientists and spiritual masters, concerning the subject of devotion and the Lord. Subsequently, many theories have emerged with conclusions, yet even to date, no single conclusive result had emerged from these discussions. The truth can be realised only through the divine grace of the Lord and the elevated souls and never through argumentative reasoning, which could prevent the devotee from practicing devotion. There are many examples of court cases that have been won by lawyers based on evidence presented in front of a judge and jury, leading to the false imprisonment of innocent persons or the release of offenders. Similarly, even if a dispute gives victory to one or the other party involved, this triumph does not necessarily lead to the truth.

Furthermore, the *Bhagwad Gita* (3.26) states, "A true wise man, who is always immersed in the joy of the Self, should not disturb the minds of those who, out of ignorance, act just to fulfil their materialistic desires. Instead, he should encourage them to perform certain actions that will naturally lead them to the path of devotion for the Lord."

"People who are mystified by the influence of the three qualities of nature become attached to those qualities and the kinds of actions arising naturally from their confused thought process. But a true wise man should not say anything to unsettle their minds." (*Bhagwad Gita* 3.29)

Hence, one should not attempt to unsettle another person's honest and sincere views. Alternatively, one ought to give him the opportunity to follow what he considers right. What one man considers to be well-established by reason can easily be shaken by another more intelligent man. Therefore, one should not waste time over fruitless discussions. Instead, one should devote oneself completely to one's spiritual master and to the Lord and with a sincere spirit, one should practice constant remembrance of Him. Sacred love can be attained by the practice of devotion, not by argument.

Sutra 76

|| *bhaktiśāstrāṇi mananīyāni tadudbodhakakarmāṇi karaṇīyāni* ||

Devotional scriptures should be discussed and meditated upon and only those actions should be performed which increase the spirit of devotion.

There is a saying in Sanskrit:

yasmiñśāstre purāṇe vā haribhaktirna dṛśyate
śrotavyaṁ naiva tacchāstraṁ yadi brahma svayaṁ vadet

> "One should never listen to any scripture that does not prominently feature descriptions of Krishn and devotion for Him, even if that scripture is recited by Brahma himself."

This aphorism states that the scriptures which speak about devotion are to be discussed and meditated upon. Sacred love manifests itself by the study of devotional scriptures, by learning the teachings of spiritual masters, by listening to their devotional talks and by practicing their instructions. The preceding aphorisms mention all the prohibitions for a sincere devotee. Here, Sage Narad clearly states that an aspirant needs to study only those scriptures which are on the subject of devotion. If one starts to read the scriptures on the paths of knowledge, action or disciplined contemplation, one will be misguided and this will lead to confusion and heated disputes. A person may present himself as a devotee, but after studying the path of action, he may perform social work to gain prestige and reputation in society. Although his actions may be praiseworthy, they may not increase his love for the Lord. He may spend more time contemplating his social work rather than thinking about offering the work to the Lord, who is the Master of his soul.

When a person becomes a devotee, it is essential for him to continue on his path, rather than diverting his mind and not fulfilling his purpose. Reading the devotional scriptures and meditating upon them will encourage a spiritual aspirant in his practice, and consequently, his actions will eventually lead him to the Lord.

In the *Srimad Bhagwatam,* the Lord mentions the actions which enhance devotion:

Whoever wants to be devoted to Me should hear My stories with great faith, glorify Me through song, venerate Me with firm attachment and praise Me with poetry. He should have great love for serving Me, and with his entire body, he should offer his obeisances to Me. He should worship My devotees even more than He worships Me, and he should see Me in all beings. He should dedicate every limb of his body to Me. He should sing about My glories. He should offer his heart and mind unto Me and renounce all ulterior desires. He should give up his wealth, enjoyments and happiness for Me and whatever rituals he performs or charity he gives, he should do for Me. Sacred love for Me awakens in the hearts of those who observe these devotional practices and offer their very selves to Me. And for those who have attained that sacred love, what else remains to be attained?" (*Srimad Bhagwatam* 11.19.20-24)

Sutra 77

|| sukhaduḥkhecchālābhādityakte kāle pratīkṣyamāṇe kṣaṇārdhamapi vyarthaṁ na neyam ||

Even a fraction of a second should not be wasted in attaining that favourable time when a devotee has liberated himself from the troubles of pain, desires, wealth, and so forth.

In this aphorism, Sage Narad says that a devotee should eagerly anticipate the time when all the emotions related to material happiness no longer affect him. Usually a person has desires for objects he has yet to attain. When his desires are fulfilled, this stage is known as profit, and thereafter, he becomes happy. As soon as he loses the profit, he feels sadness and despair, and the same situation occurs when his desires are not fulfilled. The aspirant should await the time when emotional highs and lows do not affect him. This stage does not come so effortlessly, and one can only reach this level by performing spiritual practice. Here, Sage Narad strongly suggests that one should not waste even a fraction of a second to reach this stage.

Usually, people have a perception that one should practice devotion when one is old. These persons may also feel that many other aspirations should be fulfilled prior to entering the path of devotion. In response, Kabir says:

> You can find yourself in the jaws of death, in the twinkling of an eye. Still you make no time for adoring the Lord. Do not say, "It is the springtime of my life. Let me enjoy myself and leave worship for the winter of old age." Who's to say you will live that long? The sword of death swings above your head. Love Him now.

In the *Vairagya Shatak,* Bhartrihari states, "While one is still young and healthy, one should begin working towards the ultimate goal (instead of postponing spiritual practice for the end of life). Of what use is it to begin digging a well when the house is already burning down?" The desires of a man are never fulfilled, and even if they are partially rewarded, they bring in their train of new wants and desires, and man diverts his time and energy to satisfy them. Therefore, even the least amount of time should not be wasted without practicing devotion:

kṣaṇārdhaṁ kṣemārthaṁ pibata śukagāthātulasudhām

> "Do not waste half a second! Just drink the nectar of Krishn's holy acts, which emanates from the mouth of the great saint Shukdev." (*Padma Puran*, *Srimad Bhagwatam Mahatmya*)

When it comes to devotion, Sage Narad encourages one not to indulge in idleness. This advice is very precious for a spiritual aspirant because there are no austerities he can perform to capture the time he has lost once it passes. Therefore, one should always be alert in one's spiritual practice. A devotee can chant the Holy Name and when he needs a change in his practice, he can listen to the pastimes of the Lord. If he is satisfied with hearing, he can read the pastimes of the Lord. If he feels contented with reading, he can meet with other devotees and discuss the glories of Lord Krishn. To please the Lord, the devotee is free to indulge in any of the practices mentioned in the scriptures. Anytime is favourable to practice devotion, and one should do so with the utmost dedication and love. The practice of devotion should become so inherent in a devotee that he is unable to survive without it. The devotee should always be attentive in his effort to achieve his goal. Once he attains his goal, he will become free from the dualities of happiness and misery, gain and loss, desire and lack of desire, and so forth.

Sutra 78

|| *ahiṁsāsatyaśaucadayāstikyādicāritryāṇi paripālanīyāni* ||

The devotee should cultivate virtues such as non-violence, truthfulness, cleanliness, compassion, faith in the existence of the Lord, and so forth.

The 76th aphorism advised the aspirant to perform only those actions which increase the spirit of devotion. To nurture the growth of a devotee, this aphorism discerns five special codes of conduct. Often, in the name of devotion, people say that the primary object is to cultivate devotion and not the good qualities that are necessary on the devotinal path. If the devotee lacks the more refined qualities such as non-violence, truthfulness, cleanliness, compassion, faith in the existence of the Lord, and so forth, he may excuse it by saying that at least he is a devotee and this is the most important thing. An individual may believe that as a devotee he can commit any amount of sin because he is protected. This statement is not correct. These divine qualities are part and parcel of devotees.

When an aspirant practices devotion, the celestial qualities imbue him like the rays of divinity, removing negative tendencies, just as the bright rays of the sun remove darkness. If worldly thoughts and bad qualities are growing in the aspirant, he only regresses in his progress, and he is gradually enveloped in darkness like the Earth at the setting of the sun. The great souls are living examples of these noble qualities. Here, Sage Narad elaborates on those divine qualities:

1. Non-violence: Non-violence means non-injury to anyone by one's actions, thoughts or deeds. Each person is part and parcel of the Lord and He resides in everyone. Therefore harming another is the same as harming the Lord, and for this reason, a sincere devotee cannot possibly think of hurting anyone. People who are selfish or jealous by nature usually hurt others by their thoughts, words or actions. Sometimes, even devotees are critical of other devotees or those who belong to different spiritual schools as well as those who do not believe in the Lord. This is a very counter-productive attitude for a devotee to adopt because if he starts to dislike others and becomes envious of anyone, he may not be able to meditate on his Lord. Instead, he is likely to meditate on the negativity of his feelings

towards others. Therefore, he should refrain from harming anyone by his thoughts, words or deeds.

2. Truthfulness: One can have knowledge and understanding of a subject, but this does not imply that the subject matter is correct. A man who pursues spiritual life should be truthful to the core, and his actions, words and thoughts should reflect his values. One should not waste a moment on any untruthful matter, and one should never act in a dishonest manner. A devotee should exemplify the truth by his action, speech and thought, and this practice becomes a blissful way of life for him as well as for those he inspires.

3. Cleanliness: Cleanliness does not mean outer hygiene only. Here, one should focus on internal cleanliness, for example maintenance of one's community, home and body as well as purification of one's mind and thoughts. When a devotee begins his spiritual life, the goal is to purify his heart so that only the Lord can reside there and this is not possible if it is impure. Hence, an aspirant should not harbour hypocrisy, hostility, pride, jealousy, grief, sinful thoughts, worldly thoughts, worldly attachments, and so forth.

4. Compassion: Compassion is the feeling of restlessness at the sight of human misery. This sentiment should always be cultivated for each and every creature throughout one's existence, and action that may cause suffering to others should not be practiced. An example of such compassion is found in the *Chaitanya Charitamrit* (7.136-137): "There once was a man named Vasudev. He was a jewel of a man but still he suffered from leprosy. His body was covered with wounds and in those wounds, parasites lived. Whenever a worm fell out of his body, the compassionate Vasudev lovingly picked it up and placed it back."

5. Faith in the existence of the Lord: Without faith, one cannot even walk. When a person walks, he has faith that the ground will support his weight and he has assurance that his legs will have the energy to carry him. Faith is the very essence of life, and this world is resting on faith. People have faith in each other, and even if a devotee loses hope in the world, he can focus his faith on the Lord. Faith in the existence of the Lord is the most important belief one needs to have in one's devotional practice. Sometimes, devotees run in many different directions searching for answers, trying to stabilize themselves in their practice, which can divert them from cultivating one-pointedness in their devotion. In the *Bhagwad Gita* (9.22), the Lord states that He supplies all that a sincere devotee needs in his devotional life. Therefore, those who have this assurance have no

reason to divert themselves. Lack of conviction in the Lord's existence leads to instability in the aspirant's devotion, therefore he is not able to rely on Him and he doubts in the capability of His powers.

The *Vishnu Puran* gives a perfect example of an elevated devotee who demonstrates such courage and sincerity on the path of devotion. Prahlad became a devotee of the Lord, but his father, a demon named Hiranyakashipu, was against his son's practice. On the command of Prahlad's father, thousands of demons marched furiously with their weapons to kill him. Prahlad knew his conviction would prevent the weapons from causing any harm to him because he believed that his Lord resided in these weapons, in the demons and in everything created by Him. Astonishingly, the weapons had no affect on Prahlad even though they struck him hard.

Hiranyakashipu tried many techniques to kill Prahlad. He was thrown into a fire but he did not burn. Prahlad's father sent the female destructive goddess Kritya to kill him, yet Prahlad survived. Hiranyakashipu asked his son if his Lord existed in a pillar near them. Prahlad declared, "Yes! My Lord is present everywhere. He is present even in this pillar." Hiranyakashipu took out his sword to strike the pillar. To defend the honour of His dear devotee, the Lord manifested Himself from the pillar. Therefore, this aphorism encourages devotees to constantly maintain the highest level of faith and to cultivate virtues that will continue to develop their conviction in the Lord's existence.

Sutra 79

|| *sarvadā sarvabhāvena niścintitairbhagavāneva bhajanīyaḥ* ||

One who is free from doubts should always and wholeheartedly practice sweet remembrance of the Lord whilst performing any action (a process which is known as *bhajan*) by giving up all other thoughts.

An aspirant who sincerely cultivates virtues such as non-violence, truthfulness, cleanliness, compassion, faith in the existence of the Lord, and so forth, and knows of the Lord's glories, must remember Him in his thoughts and actions, whether they are spiritual or worldly. Lord Shiv says in the *Ramcharitmanas*, "O Uma! One who has truly known Ram likes only to do His *bhajan*, nothing else."

The aspirant should engage himself in the practice of *bhajan* and offer his mind and heart to the Lord. Without this submission, the aspirant's practice becomes a matter of duty. Love never leaves the lover and the heart and mind start to think about the beloved constantly, nothing else. Hence, giving up worldly attachments and therefore worldly thoughts, one can become a devoted and faithful wife to the beloved Lord. The poet Sundar Das conveys his personal love for the Lord, which illustrates this sentiment:

patihisuň prem hoy patihisuň nem hoy
patihisuň ćhem hoy patihisuň ras hai
pati hi hai jagya-jog pati hi hai rasbhog
patihīsuň miṭai sog, patihīko jat hai
patihīko gyān-dhyān, patihīko punna-dān
pati hi hai tīrth-snān patihiko mat hai
pati binu pati nāhi pati binu gati nāhi
'sundar' sakal bidhi ek pativrat hai

> "My Husband is my Love, my Husband is my Religion, my Husband is my Welfare and He is sweetness personified. My Husband is my Spiritual Practice, My Husband is my Enjoyment; only my Husband can dissolve my sorrows, He is my only Refuge. My Husband is my Pilgrimage and my Ritual Bath, my Husband is my Heart. I have no beloved but my Husband, I have no way or goal but my Husband. He is the most beautiful in every way and I am dedicated to Him alone." (*Vrajwasi Poetry*)

10

Union with the Beloved

Sutra 80

|| *sa kīrtyamānaḥ śīghramevāvirbhavati anubhāvayati bhaktān* ||

Being thus enchanted by love, the Lord reveals Himself and blesses devotees with sweet realisation.

According to the previous and present aphorism, when an aspirant performs *bhajan* (sweet rememberance whilst performing any action) with dedication and chants the Lord's Name with love every moment of his life, the Lord Himself appears and blesses the devotee with sweet realisation.

sagunahi agunahi nahiṅ kaćhu bhedā
gāvahi muni purān budh bedā
agun arūp alakh aj joī
bhagat prem bas sagun so hoī

> "The wise men, sages and scriptures all say that the Unmanifest Absolute and the Manifest Lord are One. That selfsame attributeless Ultimate Reality appears with form and qualities and is brought under control by the love of His lovers." (*Vrajwasi Poetry*)

In stages, the *Narad Bhakti Sutra* beautifully unravels how the Lord appears before His dearest devotees. Even the demons are able to have an audience with Lord Krishn.

The Lord manifests Himself in five different ways:

1. The Lord manifests and disappears
2. The Lord manifests and stays for some time
3. The Lord manifests, converses with the aspirant and fulfils his desires
4. The Lord manifests with His associates and the aspirant watches Their play

5. The Lord manifests with His associates and the aspirant participates in Their play

Of these five different levels, the last one is the most important because at this stage, the aspirant becomes one of the Lord's personal associates and performs actions in His eternal abode.

Sutra 81

|| *trisatyasya bhaktireva garīyasī bhaktireva garīyasī* ||

According to three truths, the path of devotion alone is the greatest of all.

Here Sage Narad says *trisatya*, which means the three truths in Sanskrit. The three truths can either refer to the past, present and future, or the body, speech and mind. As established by the scriptures and by realised souls, the past, present and future declare that devotion was the supreme path, is still the supreme path and shall always be the superior path.

An aspirant on the path of devotion uses his body to perform devotional practice, glorifies the Lord with his speech and meditates upon Him with his mind and thus attains Him easily. The aspirant can also use the body, speech and mind to perform charitable works (the path of action) or *raj yog*, and so forth. But the scriptures clearly state that devotion is the easiest and greatest way because it is a direct path. Narad declares that the three truths confirm the path of devotion as the greatest of all paths, and the scriptures also agree with Sage Narad's statement. "Abandon all other methods and take exclusive shelter of the path of devotion. Be devoted to devotion; be devoted to devotion, for through devotion, all perfections are achieved. Indeed, there is nothing that cannot be achieved through devotion." (*Tripad Vibhuti Narayan Upanishad*)

Sutra 82

|| guṇa-māhātmyāsakti-rūpāsakti-pūjāsakti-smaraṇāsakti-dāsyāsakti-sakhyāsakti-vātsalyāsakti-kāntāsakti-ātmanivedanāsakti-tanmayatāsakti-paramavirahāsaktirūpā ekādaśadhā bhavati ||

Although the path to the Lord is one, it is expressed in eleven different forms: attachment (1) to the Lord's virtues and glories, (2) to His beauty, (3) to His worship, (4) to His remembrance, (5) to serving Him, (6) to loving Him as His friend, (7) to caring for Him as a parent, (8) to caring for Him as His wife, (9) to complete self-surrender unto Him, (10) to being in a state of absorption in Him and (11) to the supreme anguish of separation from Him.

In this aphorism, Sage Narad reveals eleven types of devotion, although fundamentally devotion is one path. The great souls who reach the highest stage of devotion possess one or some of these eleven types of attachments, just as the *gopis* of Vraj did. One should choose one or as many of these attachments as one can, and with the guidance of a spiritual master, cultivate the resulting relationship with the Lord. The process to connect to the Lord should be understood clearly. In many religions, people chant the Lord's Holy Name on beads, but whilst chanting the mind wanders towards worldly affairs. People are also easily distracted by external noises. These diversions show that the attachment is there for the other activities and not for the Holy Name or for the Lord.

Attachment gives rise to one-pointedness. This type of single-mindedness can be demonstrated by the example of a playful child. When the child is reluctantly called back from playtime with his friends to complete his study, he is unable to focus on his schoolwork because his mind redirects itself back to the game he was playing with them, as if he never left their company. He tries to find an opportunity to sneak out. In the same way, there are many other earthly attachments such as attachment to money, to status, to family, to one's appearance, and so forth, but Sage Narad's wisdom in the form of these eleven types of devotion becomes the spiritual antidote to the bitterness of those worldly attachments.

Narad elaborates on these eleven forms in more detail:

1. Attachment to the Lord's virtues and glories: One's eyes and ears can be attracted towards anything. When one is charmed by another's beauty or impressed by his work, especially when one

hears his praises, one becomes enthusiastic to see and meet that person. In the same way, Sage Narad reveals that when an aspirant is eager to know the Lord, he should attach himself by listening to His virtues and glories. The *Srimad Bhagwatam* (4.20.24) states, "Oh Lord! I do not desire to merge into You, for in that state, I cannot taste the ambrosia of Your lotus feet. I would rather prefer to be blessed with a million ears with which I can listen to the glories of Your lotus feet from Your great devotees." The *gopis* felt this strong attachment to the dark-coloured Boy Krishn, and it was so intense that they proclaimed all black-coloured things to be dangerous. In the anguish of separation from Krishn, an angry Radha told the *gopis*, "So let Us give up all friendship with Krishn, but We cannot live without hearing about Him." (*Srimad Bhagwatam* 10.47.17)

2. Attachment to His beauty: After hearing the glories and virtues of a person, one becomes eager to see and meet him. Sage Narad says that the devotee should attach himself to the Lord's beauty. To see someone in the heart is very difficult. To see someone with closed eyes can be possible because one can internally visualise an image of that person. But to see someone with eyes wide open (in his absence) and to create that internal image externally is impossible unless one has attachment with that person. When attachment is not there, he cannot meditate on someone's beauty even if it is in front of him. Beauty has existed in the world since time immemorial and humans are naturally drawn to beauty. Therefore, this form of devotion is pleasurable for them. In the *Srimad Bhagwatam* (10.19.16), "The young cowherd women loved watching Krishn come home, since for them, a moment without Him was like a hundred ages." When Lord Ram injured the demon Surpanaka, she ran to her brothers Khar and Dushan for protection. Upon seeing her injuries, her brothers became furious and went in search of Lord Ram to kill Him. Just by seeing the Lord's beauty they forgot everything and declared:

hum bhari janam sunahu sab bhāī dekhī nahiṅ asi sundaratāī
jadyapi bhaginī kīnhi kurūpā badha lāyak nahiṅ puruṣh anūpā

> "In our whole lives we have never seen beauty like Yours. Although You have taken away our sister's beauty (by cutting off her nose) we cannot bring ourselves to hurt You, for to do so would be to harm Your incomparable attractiveness." (*Ramcharitmanas, Aranya Kand*)

3. Attachment to His worship: Just seeing a person whom one has affection for does not necessarily make it easier for one to express

one's feelings towards that person. So Sage Narad says, after attachment to the beauty of the Lord, one should start to serve Him by worshipping Him. One should worship Him like Uddhav. "When he was five years old, Uddhav used to dress, serve and worship dolls, believing them to be Krishn. Uddhav was so absorbed in his adoration that when his mother called him to eat breakfast, he did not want to come." (*Srimad Bhagwatam* 3.2.2)

4. Attachment to His remembrance: When one worships the Lord, one should connect oneself to the Lord by remembering Him with one-pointedness, without being distracted by worldly affairs.

vipado naiva vipadaḥ sampado naiva sampadaḥ
vipad vismaraṇaṁ viṣṇoḥ sampannārāyaṇasmrtiḥ

"Worldly pain is not real pain, nor worldly wealth real wealth. To forget the Lord is the only true misery and to remember Him is true wealth." (*Sanskrit Proverb*)

5. Attachment to serving Him: The soul is an eternal servant of the Lord. An aspirant should develop an attitude akin to that of the charioteer Daarun. One day, whilst fanning Lord Krishn, Daarun began to feel overwhelmed and blessed by serving the Lord in this way. He was fully aware that there were many devotees who wanted to be in his position, yet he was the fortunate one designated with this service. At the same time, Daarun tried to stop these sentiments of arrogance or pride, which he knew would become obstacles in his devotion, by reminding himself that he was merely a servant of his Master. He felt that by performing this service, he should not be seeking his personal happiness. Instead, he should ascertain whether his Beloved is happy or not. In the Lord's pleasure rests the servant's joy. Any sincere servant who practices devotion should have this nature and regard the Lord as his Master.

6. Attachment to loving Him as a friend: When the devotee becomes a servant, the Lord tries to become his Friend. When Lord Krishn incarnated on this Earth, He used to deliberately lose games to make His friends happy. A servant is someone who always keeps himself far, but friendship brings him closer to the Lord. In Lord Ram's era, His brother Bharat said, "I have realised the grace of my Lord in my heart, for He would make Himself the loser of the game, although it is I who should have lost it." (*Ramcharitmanas*)

7. Attachment to caring for Him as a parent: Initially, the relationship of a devotee with His Lord is that of a servant, which intensifies and reaches the second stage, where the Lord and the devotee become

friends. Sage Narad says that when one loves and cares for the Beloved as a baby, it is known as the third phase and it is a much deeper relationship with the Lord. Mother Yashoda and Nand *Baba*[61] had this love for Lord Krishn. When Lord Krishn incarnated on Earth to kill Hiranyaksh, all the oceans could not fill His hair follicles. This was not the case when the same Lord Krishn came as Yashoda's Child. "In His incarnation as Varah, all the waters of the seven seas could not even fill the Lord's pores. But the same Lord, when He came as Yashoda's Son, bathed in just as much water as His mother could hold in the palms of her hands." (*Krishn Karnamrit* 2.27)

8. Attachment to caring for Him as His wife: In aphorism 66, Narad mentioned that an aspirant can devote himself as a wife to serve the Lord. Here Narad says that a devotee (male or female) can cultivate a more profound attachment to Him, deeper than a parental one, by serving Him as His wife.

9. Attachment to complete self-surrender unto Him: This attachment means to offer all that one possesses to please one's Lord.

10. Attachment to being in a state of absorption in Him: When Lord Krishn disappeared from the *Raas Mandal*, the *gopis* of Vraj forgot everything, including their own identities, and started to behave as if they were Krishn. Some *gopis* were wearing yellow shawls and acting like Krishn, whilst another *gopi* started to play the flute, thinking she was the Lord. Fully immersed in His love, the *gopis* were imitating Krishn's plays, thinking that they had become Him. Absorption in Him comes when, as a lover, the devotee forgets himself.

11. Attachment to the supreme anguish of separation from Him: There are two types of separation: one, where a devotee calls Him and He appears and then disappears and two, where the devotee feels separation in the presence of the Lord. In the tenth canto of the *Srimad Bhagwatam*, Lord Krishn was playing a water game with His wives, and all of a sudden the wives started to weep. Although Krishn was in their presence, the wives felt that He was not there.

Once, Radha and Krishn were sitting together. All of a sudden Radha felt the anguish of extreme separation from Her Beloved and started crying, "Krishn! Krishn! Krishn!" She fell unconscious thereafter.

---

[61] A *baba* in this context is a father.

Seeing the condition of Radha, Krishn felt separation and started crying, "Radha! Radha! Radha!" He too, became unconscious in separation.

When Radha regained Her consciousness, She found Krishn unconscious, so She started to weep again until She fainted. This cycle continued until Radha's closest friend Lalita came to intervene.

When one's desires are fulfilled, the yearning for the object of desire disappears. Hence, to maintain this longing, the sentiment of profound separation is necessary in devotion. Therefore, spiritual masters like Sage Narad always encourage the aspirants to cultivate an attachment where they feel intense separation in love.

Sutra 83

|| *ityevaṁ vadanti janajalpanirbhayā ekamatāḥ kumāra-vyāsa-śuka-śāṇḍilya-garga-viṣṇu-kauṇḍinya-śeṣo'ddhavāruṇi-bali-hanumad-vibhīṣaṇādayo bhaktyācāryāḥ* ||

Hence, all the teachers of devotion such as Kumar, Vyasdev, Shukdev, Shandilya, Garg, Vishnu, Kaundinya, Shesh, Uddhav, Aruni, Bali, Hanuman, Vibhishan, and so forth, who are unafraid of others and their idle gossiping, deliver their undisputed opinion.

To strengthen his opinion and highlight the significance of his teachings, Sage Narad refers to many other eminent teachers, who were also practitioners of devotion. He resolutely declares the path of devotion to be the most supreme. Although there were subtle differences in the philosophy of each one of these teachers, their path was the same. Few wrote their own works but many of the teachers became role models by their personal devotion.

The Sanat Kumars were constantly engaged in chanting the Holy Name. To date, they are still known as princes among devotees. In the *Purans*, the author Vyasdev declared devotion to be the supreme path, and his principal *Puran*, the *Srimad Bhagwatam*, is the most ripe and nectarean fruit of devotion. From his lips, Shukdev spoke the *Srimad Bhagwatam*, which imparts the real bliss of devotion. Sage Shandilya has written devotional scriptures and established himself on this path.

Sage Garg is the founder of astrology, but his widely-known scripture, the *Garg Samhita,* established his firm belief and understanding of this path. In the *Moksh Dharm* section of the *Mahabharat Shantiparv*, one can read about Narayan (or Vishnu, an incarnation of Lord Krishn), who was a great pioneer on the path of devotion and Vishnu was also Sage Narad's teacher. Kaundinya became illustrious because he attained perfection by absorbing himself in the Lord through the practice of meditation.

Narayan rests on a bed made of the coils of the multi-headed snake Anant-shesh (Shesh). The eleven cobra heads of Shesh protect the Lord's head. With his many mouths, Shesh is always engaged in chanting and glorifying the Lord. He incarnated as Lakshman, Lord Ram's brother, to propagate devotion by being an exemplary devotee himself. Uddhav was the most intimate friend of Krishn. The

Srimad Bhagwatam mentions that upon Krishn's return to His eternal abode, He gave all the required knowledge of devotion and other subject matters to Uddhav, so that Uddhav could spread devotion in the world after the Lord's departure.

Aruni, a great sage, who is mentioned in the *Chandogya Upanishad* (6.9.4), was a devotee of the Absolute (the unmanifested, formless Lord). King Bali practiced self-surrender to the Lord and in return, the Lord became the king's palace gatekeeper. Hence, Bali received an audience with the Lord every time he entered and exited his palace. Hanuman's devotion as a humble servant is exemplary all over the world. A most knowledgeable devotee, Hanuman constantly chanted Lord Ram's Name and engaged his senses in hearing his Beloved's glories. Being pleased with Vibhishan's devotion, the Lord became his dear Friend.

In this aphorism, Sage Narad used the words "and so forth." He only named a few distinguished teachers of devotion but there were many more inspirational figures who created milestones on this supreme path. Even to date, the world is still a beneficiary of the finest exemplars of devotion.

Sutra 84

|| ya idaṁ nāradaproktaṁ śivānuśāsanaṁ viśvasiti śraddhate sa bhaktimān bhavati sa preṣṭhaṁ labhate sa preṣṭhaṁ labhata iti ||

He who has belief and firm faith in the instructions taught in this doctrine by Sage Narad, attains his beloved Lord, O yes! He surely attains his beloved Lord.

Finally, after giving his definitive exposition on the subject of devotion, Sage Narad unravels the conclusion of his doctrine. He states that those who believe and have unwavering faith on these auspicious aphorisms attain the Lord as their Beloved. In his teachings, Sage Narad is not overpowering or harsh; his way is simple, easily understandable and can be followed by anyone without difficulty. Nowadays, it seems that the path of devotion has become very intricate and confusing. There can be a tendency to be distracted by politics or philosophical contention among sects, though the essence of the path is actually extremely simple.

So here, Narad tries to show the path of devotion in a straightforward manner, where the spiritual aspirant needs no prerequisites. By taking the shelter of a spiritual master who has a real grasp of the *Narad Bhakti Sutra* and who understands the path of devotion, anyone and everyone can be a student. This is beauty of Narad's teachings.

In this concluding aphorism, Sage Narad states that two things are necessary, belief and sincere faith, and if both are present, the aspirant can begin his devotional practice, which he must perform earnestly. On the surface, belief and faith can appear to mean the same. Usually, belief comes from one's personal understanding, whether it is true or not. But here, belief means conviction in Narad's instructions and faith is the root of this conviction. The scriptures say that devotion should be practiced with assurance and reverence. One can realise the Lord on the other paths (the path of knowledge, the path of action and the path of disciplined contemplation), but Narad states that by following his teachings on the path of devotion, the Lord will be realised as the aspirants' Beloved, which is the highest form of devotion. In other words, the Lord is not worshipped from a distance, in His regal form; here, there is a reciprocal loving relationship between the devotee and his Lord. Krishn, who is the supreme object of life, is dear to His devotee, just as His devotee is to Him.

In the *Srimad Bhagwatam* (9.4.68), Lord Krishn says, "My loving devotees are My heart and I am their Heart. They know nothing but Me, and I know none but them." The beloved Lord thus pays the ultimate tribute to those who have surrendered to Him by stating, "Wherever the great souls go, I follow them with the hope that the dust of their feet may fall upon Me and purify Me." Thereby, the Lord confirms that devotion alone can make Him fall in love with His devotees, and in return, Lord Krishn offers the most supreme nectar imaginable; He drowns with them in the bottomless ocean of His infinite love.

****

"But I have heard from the mouths of sages that Love makes the impossible possible. Love experiences what reason cannot know, and the heart can see visions that the eyes cannot see . . . May this book open our eyes of love, forever."

|| Radhe Radhe ||

Glossary

Aarta: The troubled.

Adhikari: Whom this doctrine is meant for.

Amrit: Nectar.

Ananyas: Exclusivity.

Anartha-nivritti: Cessation of harmful habits and cleansing of bad qualities.

Anubhav: That innermost experience, which never changes.

Anuraag: Loving attachment.

Api: Unintentional.

Arth: Wealth.

Artharthi: One who desires material benefit.

Asakti: Deep attachment.

Asans (in *Raj Yog*): Physical postures.

Ashram: A solitary place of living with the most basic facilities, particularly suitable for austere aspirants who want to focus on their spiritual practice.

Asthang Yog: The eight stages to liberation as described by the *Patanjali Yog Sutra*.

Atmaram: One who is completely absorbed in the joy of one's realisation of the Lord.

Atmarati: Taking delight in the Self.

Baba: Father.

Bhaav: Extreme maturity of deep attachment (*asakti*).

Bhagwat-dharm: The path of devotional practice.

Bhajan: Sweet rememberance in the performance of any action.

Bhakti Yog: The path of devotion.

Bhakti: Devotion.

Bheda: Divide.

Bhittih Bhedanat: That which breaks up.

Bhog: Offering to the Lord, for His happiness.

Brahman: The Lord without a form, also known as the Absolute.

Brahmin: A priest of the highest caste.

Chapatis: Indian flat bread.

Dadamyaham: I supply.

Dharm: Religious duties.

Dhyan: Meditation.

Ghat: Wide flight of steps leading to Indian riverbank.

Gopis: Cowherd girls of Vrindavan.

Gunas: The threefold qualities of nature (*sattva*, *rajas* and *tamas*).

Guru: A spiritual master or a spiritual guide.

Gyan Yog: The path of knowledge.

Gyan: Knowledge.

Gyani: Knowledgeable.

Jigyasu: Inquisitive.

Kaam: Lust/Desire.

Kaliyug: The name of the present age in Hinduism, also known as the age of demise. It is the last of the four great ages (*Satyug, Dwapar Yug, Treta Yug and Kaliyug*).

Kamya: The action one performs to fulfil one's desires.

Karm Yog: The path of action.

Karm: Action.

Kriyas: Cleansing techniques.

Kund: A sacred pool of holy water.

Maansik: Mental.

Madhur Sangeet: Melody.

Madhurya Ras: The profound taste of pure love (not sexual in nature) between a lover and the Lord. In *bhakti yog*, this stage is the highest form of devotion to the Lord.

Madhurya: Sweetness.

Mahabharat: One of the great Hindu epics and it chronicles the battle between the Pandavs and the Kauravs. The *Bhagwad Gita* is a section of this epic.

Mantra: A string of Sanskrit syllables or words which is used in prayer and which contains the full power of the divine person (or persons) whose name it contains.

Maya: Illusion.

Naimittik: The action one performs according to instructions.

Nastik: Atheist.

Niraag Vakta: A speaker who is immersed in divine love and who gives talks without the use music as such, except when he sings the Holy Name.

Nishid: The action one performs that is prohibited.

Nistha: Steadiness in *bhajan*.

Nitya: The action one performs daily.

Niyams: Observances.

Pitar: One's living parents as well as one's deceased ancestors.

Pranayam: Breathing techniques.

Prayojan: Purpose.

Prem: Sacred love for the Lord.

Puja: Worship.

Pushtimarg: A school of *Vaishnavism*, founded by the spiritual master Vallabhacharya.

Raag: Attachment.

Raas Mandal: A place where the Divine Dance was performed between Lord Krishn, Radha and the rest of the *gopis*.

Raj Yog: The path of disciplined contemplation; a practice to still the wandering mind.

Rajas: The quality of passion, activity and restlessness.

Rajasik: Passionate.

Rasayan: Essence.

Ruchi: Consistent delight in every item of practice.

Sad-gati: Deliverance.

Sambandh: Relationship.

Sankhya: One of the six orthodox schools of Hindu philosophy, which does not believe in the existence of a God.

Sankirtan: A collective singing of the Lord's Names.

Saraag Vakta: A materially-minded speaker who gives his talks using music.

Sattva: The quality of purity, mental stillness and clarity.

Sattvik: Pure.

Shaligram Shila: The black stone form of Krishn, found at the Gandaki River in Nepal.

Shyam: Dark or more specifically, lovely and black with a bluish tinge.

Siddh: One who has attained the ultimate stage of devotion for the Lord.

Siddhi: A state of perfection reached when one has attainted the Lord.

Siddhis: Supernatural powers gained by a devotee after a certain stage of his devotional practice.

Sutras: Aphorisms or sayings.

Swaati: A star in *Vedic* astrology.

Tamas: The quality of ignorance and inertia.

Tamasik: Slothful or dark.

Tantra: A practice of religious rituals written in the scriptures.

Tirths: Holy lands or crossing-over points between the material and spiritual worlds.

Trisatya: Three truths.

Tulsi: Holy Basil plant and in Lord Vishnu's abode (*Vaikunth*), she is one of His wives. The scriptures mention that Lord Krishn accepts offerings made with the leaf of a *tulsi* plant.

Vahamyaham: I carry.

Vaikunth: Lord Vishnu's abode.

Vaishnavism: Religious movement devoted to Lord Vishnu/Krishn.

Vaishnavs: Devotees of Lord Vishnu/Krishn.

Vishay: Subject matter.

Yagya: A ritual of offering made to the Lord (or the gods).

Yams: Restraints.

Yog: The Sanskrit word for yoga, which means to yoke or join.

Yogi: One who practices one of the paths of *yog*.

A list of the 84 Aphorisms in Sanskrit

1. *athāto bhaktiṁ vyākhyāsyāmaḥ*
2. *sā tvasmin paramapremarūpā*
3. *amṛtasvarūpā ca*
4. *yallabdhvā pumān siddho bhavati amṛto bhavati tṛpto bhavati*
5. *yat prāpya na kiñcid vāñchati na śocati na dveṣṭi na ramate notsāhī bhavati*
6. *yatjñātvā matto bhavati stabdho bhavati ātmarāmo bhavati*
7. *sā na kāmayamānā nirodharūpatvāt*
8. *nirodhastu lokavedavyāpāranyāsaḥ*
9. *tasminnananyatā tadvirodhiṣūdāsīnatā ca*
10. *anyāśrayāṇāṁ tyāgo'nanyatā*
11. *lokavedeṣu tadanukūlācaraṇaṁ tadvirodhiṣūdāsīnatā*
12. *bhavatu niścayadārḍhyādūrdhvaṁ śāstrarakṣaṇam*
13. *anyathā pātityaśaṅkayā*
14. *loko'pi tāvadeva bhojanādivyāpārastvāśarīradhāraṇāvadhi*
15. *tallakṣaṇāni vācyante nānāmatabhedāt*
16. *pūjādiṣvanurāga iti pārāśaryaḥ*
17. *kathādiṣviti gargaḥ*
18. *ātmaratyavirodheneti śāṇḍilyaḥ*
19. *nāradastu tadarpitākhilācāratā tadvismaraṇe paramavyākulateti*
20. *astyevamevam*
21. *yathā vrajagopikānām*
22. *tatrāpi na māhātmyajñānavismṛtyapavādaḥ*
23. *tadvihīnaṁ jārāṇāmiva*
24. *nāstyeva tasmiṁstatsukhasukhitvam*
25. *sā tu karmajñānayogebhyo'pyadhikatarā*
26. *phalarūpatvāt*

27. *Īśvarasyāpyabhimānadveṣitvād dainyapriyatvāc ca*
28. *tasyā jñānameva sādhanamityeke*
29. *anyonyāśrayatvamityanye*
30. *svayaṁphalarūpateti brahmakumāraḥ*
31. *rājagṛhabhojanādiṣu tathaiva dṛṣṭatvāt*
32. *na tena rājaparitoṣaḥ kṣucchāntirvā*
33. *tasmātsaiva grāhyā mumukṣubhiḥ*
34. *tasyāḥ sādhanāni gāyantyācāryāḥ*
35. *tat tu viṣayatyāgāt saṅgatyāgāc ca*
36. *avyāvṛttabhajanāt*
37. *loke'pi bhagavadguṇaśravaṇakīrtanāt*
38. *mukhyatastu mahatkṛpayaiva bhagavatkṛpāleśād vā*
39. *mahatsaṅgastu durlabho'gamyo'moghaśca*
40. *labhyate'pi tatkṛpayaiva*
41. *tasmiṁstajjane bhedābhāvāt*
42. *tadeva sādhyatāṁ tadeva sādhyatām*
43. *duḥsaṅgaḥ sarvathaiva tyājyaḥ*
44. *kāma krodha moha smṛtibhraṁśabuddhināśa sarvanāśa kāraṇatvāt*
45. *taraṅgayitā apīme saṅgāt samudrāyanti*
46. *kastarati kastarati māyāṁ? yaḥ saṅgāṁtyajati yo mahānubhāvaṁ sevate nirmamo bhavati*
47. *yo viviktasthānaṁ sevate yo lokabandhamunmūlayati nistraiguṇyo bhavati yo yogakṣemaṁ tyajati*
48. *yaḥ karmaphalaṁ tyajati karmāṇi sannyasyati tato nirdvandvo bhavati*
49. *yo vedānapi sannyasyati kevalamavicchinnānurāgaṁ labhate*
50. *sa tarati sa tarati sa lokāṁstārayati*
51. *anirvacanīyaṁ premasvarūpam*
52. *mūkāsvādanavat*

53. *prakāśate' kvāpi pātre*

54. *guṇarahitaṁ kāmanārahitaṁ pratikṣaṇa vardhamānaṁ avichhinnaṁ sūkṣmataramanubhavarūpam*

55. *tat prāpya tadevāvalokayati tadeva śṛṇoti tadeva bhāṣayati tadeva cintayati*

56. *gauṇī tridhā guṇabhedādārtādibhedād vā*

57. *uttarasmāduttarastmātpūrvapūrvā śreyāya bhavati*

58. *anyasmāt saulabhyaṁ bhaktau*

59. *pramāṇāntarasyānapekṣatvāt svayaṁ pramāṇatvāt*

60. *śāntirūpātparamānandarūpācca*

61. *lokahānau cintā na kāryā niveditātmalokavedatvāt*

62. *na tatsiddhau lokavyavahāro heyaḥ kintu phalatyāgastatsādhanaṁ ca kāryameva*

63. *strīdhananāstika caritraṁ na sravaṇīyam*

64. *abhimānadambhādikaṁ tyājyam*

65. *tadarpitākhilācāraḥ san kāmakrodhābhimānādikaṁ tasminneva karaṇīyam*

66. *trirūpabhaṅgapūrvakaṁ nityadāsyanityakāntābhajanātmakaṁ prema kāryaṁ premaiva kāryam*

67. *bhaktā ekāntino mukhyāḥ*

68. *kaṇṭhāvarodharomāñcāśrubhiḥ parasparaṁ lapamānāḥ pāvayanti kulāni pṛthivīṁ ca*

69. *tīrthīkurvanti tīrthāni sukarmīkurvanti karmāṇi sacchāstrīkurvanti śāstrāṇi*

70. *tanmayāḥ*

71. *modante pitaro nṛtyanti devatāḥ sanāthā ceyaṁ bhūrbhavati*

72. *nāsti teṣu jātividyārūpakuladhanakriyādi bhedaḥ*

73. *yatastadīyāḥ*

74. *vādo nāvalambyaḥ*

75. *bāhulyāvakāśatvād aniyatatvācca*

76. *bhaktiśāstrāṇi mananīyāni tadudbodhakakarmāṇi karaṇīyāni*

77. *sukhaduḥkhecchālābhādityakte kāle pratīkṣyamāṇe kṣaṇārdhamapi vyarthaṁ na neyam*

78. *ahiṁsāsatyaśaucadayāstikyādicāritryāṇi paripālanīyāni*

79. *sarvadā sarvabhāvena niścintitairbhagavāneva bhajanīyaḥ*

80. *sa kīrtyamānaḥ śīghramevāvirbhavati anubhāvayati bhaktān*

81. *trisatyasya bhaktireva garīyasī bhaktireva garīyasī*

82. *guṇa-māhātmyāsakti-rūpāsakti-pūjāsakti-smaraṇāsakti-dāsyāsakti-sakhyāsakti-vātsalyāsakti-kāntāsakti-ātmanivedanāsakti-tanmayatāsakti-paramavirahāsaktirūpā ekādaśadhā bhavati*

83. *ityevaṁ vadanti janajalpanirbhayā ekamatāḥ kumāra-vyāsa-śuka-śāṇḍilya-garga-viṣṇu-kauṇḍinya-śeṣo'ddhavāruṇi-bali-hanumad-vibhīṣaṇādayo bhaktyācāryāḥ*

84. *ya idaṁ nāradaproktaṁ śivānuśāsanaṁ viśvasiti śraddhate sa bhaktimān bhavati sa preṣṭhaṁ labhate sa preṣṭhaṁ labhata iti*

A list of the 84 Aphorisms in English

1. Therefore, we shall now explain devotion.
2. Devotion has been described as sacred love towards the Lord.
3. Devotion for the Lord is also like immortal nectar.
4. After obtaining devotion, the devotee becomes perfect, immortal and extremely satisfied.
5. After attaining devotion, a devotee has no desire for anything. He does not grieve or hate, nor does he delight in anything and he does not feel encouraged to do anything else.
6. After understanding devotion, the devotee becomes intoxicated. He becomes stunned in ecstasy and thus finds all joy in his Self.
7. There is no question of *kaam* (lust/desire) in devotion because devotion is attained through complete control of the senses.
8. Control or cessation means to give up all kinds of social customs and religious rituals governed by *Vedic* injunction.
9. In devotion there is cessation of everything other than one-pointedness to the Lord and indifference to things opposed to Him.
10. Discarding everything except the Lord is one-pointedness in devotion.
11. To accept only those activities of social custom and *Vedic* injunction that are favourable to devotion and to have complete indifference towards all actions which obstruct the path to the Lord.
12. One must continue to follow scriptural injunctions until one's faith is firmly established.
13. Otherwise there is every possibility of falling from the ideal.
14. Social activities, such as eating, should be followed and continued as long as the body lasts.

15. Now the characteristics of devotion will be stated according to various authoritative opinions.
16. According to Vyasdev, the son of Sage Parashar, devotion means attraction to worship.
17. According to Sage Garg, devotion is a real fondness for hearing the Lord's glories.
18. Sage Shandilya believes that devotion for the Lord results from renouncing all barriers which deviate one from taking pleasure in Him.
19. However, Narad feels that devotion consists of offering all activities to the Lord and the feeling of extreme distress by the devotee if He is forgotten.
20. Devotion is correctly described in this way alone.
21. A great example of the exact nature of this devotion is that of the *gopis*, the cowherd women of Vraj.
22. Even in the case of the *gopis*, one cannot criticize that they were not aware of the Lord's divine personality.
23. Love without the knowledge of His true nature is like an illicit affair.
24. In lust, there is a tendency for self-satisfaction, and no pleasure is derived by making the Beloved happy.
25. The path of devotion is superior to the path of action (*karm yog*), the path of knowledge (*gyan yog*) and the path of disciplined contemplation (*raj yog*).
26. Devotion is the process to attain the goal and the goal itself; devotion is the means and the end.
27. Because the Lord dislikes pride and loves humility.
28. According to some spiritual masters, devotion can only be attained through knowledge.
29. Some spiritual masters say that knowledge and devotion are dependent on each other.
30. According to the sons of Brahma (Sanak, Sanandan, Sanatan, and Sanat Kumar), devotion is its own fruit.
31. (Combined with 32)

32. For it is seen in the case of a regal palace and a meal, mere knowledge does not win the favour of the king, nor is one's hunger appeased by the sight of food.
33. Therefore, devotion alone is to be accepted by those who desire to cut all material bondages.
34. In hymns and songs, the spiritual teachers describe the means of attaining devotion.
35. Devotion is attained through renunciation of objects of sense pleasure, as well as attachments to them.
36. And through an uninterrupted offering of devotional practice to the Lord.
37. By listening to and singing His pastimes and glories, even while engaged in social life.
38. Primarily, through the grace of the great devotees, or through a little grace from the Lord.
39. The association of great souls is rarely obtained and recognized, yet it is infallible.
40. Association of great souls can be obtained through the Lord's grace alone.
41. Because the Lord and His great devotees are non-different.
42. Therefore without fail, attain that holy association alone.
43. One should avoid bad association of any kind.
44. Bad association brings lust, anger, delusion, forgetfulness of the goal and complete ruin.
45. In the beginning, these passions may remain like ripples but bad association turns them into an ocean.
46. Who overcomes delusion? He who gives up all attachment, he who serves great souls and he who gives up the idea of egotism.
47. Who can overcome delusion? He who lives in solitude, cuts off the bondages of this world, goes beyond the three qualities of nature and renounces the idea of obtaining or preserving the objects of the world.
48. Who can overcome delusion? He who gives up the effect of all actions. He who renounces all actions passes beyond duality, such as pleasure and pain, and so forth.

49. Who can overcome delusion? He who discards the *Veds* and attains uninterrupted love for the Lord.
50. He crosses over, certainly he crosses over. He even helps others cross over their delusion.
51. The nature of love is beyond words; it is indescribable.
52. It is like the taste of the mute.
53. That sacred love appears in a worthy person.
54. This sacred love is devoid of qualities, it is desireless and it increases with each moment. It is unbroken, is subtler than the subtlest and it is the form of innermost experience.
55. After the attainment of sacred love, the devotee sees nothing but love, hears only about love, speaks only of love and thinks only of love.
56. There are three kinds of secondary devotion mentioned according to the nature of the devotee.
57. Among these, each preceding category is superior to the succeeding one.
58. The Lord is easier to attain by devotion than by any other path.
59. Devotion does not depend upon any other proof because it is itself the proof.
60. The path of devotion is easier than other paths because its nature is of supreme peace and supreme bliss.
61. The devotee should not worry about worldly losses because he has surrendered himself and his temporal and spiritual interests to the Lord.
62. Until one has attained devotion, one should not discard the good worldly activities. But devotion should be practiced renouncing the fruit of those activities.
63. Talks about women (sex), wealth, non-believers and enemies are not to be heard.
64. Pride, pretence and other vices should be abandoned.
65. One should devote all actions to the Lord and direct one's desire, anger, pride, and so forth, towards Him.
66. Rising above the three categories of devotion (mentioned in aphorism 56), sacred love and sacred love alone should be

cultivated in the mood of constant service to the Lord, either as a devoted servant or wife.

67. Devotees who are exclusively attached to the Lord with one-pointedness are the finest.
68. Conversing with one another in broken words, voices choked with emotion, with bristling of their bodily hairs and tears streaming from their eyes, such fine devotees bless their families and the world also.
69. Such devotees increase the sanctity of holy places, render all actions blessed and make the scriptures more sacred.
70. For they (the finest devotees) are absorbed in the Lord.
71. On the advent of a fine devotee, his ancestors rejoice, the gods dance in joy, and Mother Earth finds a protector in him.
72. Among these primary devotees there is no distinction based upon caste, customs, physical appearance, family, wealth, profession, and the like.
73. Because they (the perfected saints and devotees) are the Lord's very own.
74. It is improper for any devotee to enter into controversy.
75. Because there is scope for many different points and none are definitive.
76. Devotional scriptures should be discussed and meditated upon and only those actions should be performed which increase the spirit of devotion.
77. Even a fraction of a second should not be wasted in attaining that favourable time when a devotee has liberated himself from the troubles of pain, desires, wealth, and so forth.
78. The devotee should cultivate virtues such as non-violence, truthfulness, cleanliness, compassion, faith in the existence of the Lord, and so forth.
79. One who is free from doubts should always and wholeheartedly practice sweet remembrance of the Lord whilst performing any action (a process which is known as *bhajan*) by giving up all other thoughts.
80. Being thus enchanted by love, the Lord reveals Himself and blesses devotees with sweet realisation.

81. According to three truths, the path of devotion alone is the greatest of all.

82. Although the path to the Lord is one, it is expressed in eleven different forms: attachment (1) to the Lord's virtues and glories, (2) to His beauty, (3) to His worship, (4) to His remembrance, (5) to serving Him, (6) to loving Him as His friend, (7) to caring for Him as a parent, (8) to caring for Him as His wife, (9) to complete self-surrender unto Him, (10) to being in a state of absorption in Him and (11) to the supreme anguish of separation from Him.

83. Hence, all the teachers of devotion such as Kumar, Vyasdev, Shukdev, Shandilya, Garg, Vishnu, Kaundinya, Shesh, Uddhav, Aruni, Bali, Hanuman, Vibhishan, and so forth, who are unafraid of others and their idle gossiping, deliver their undisputed opinion.

84. He who has belief and firm faith in the instructions taught in this doctrine by Sage Narad, attains his beloved Lord, O yes! He surely attains his beloved Lord.

Pronunciation Guide

Sanskrit Transliteration

Devanagari is the alphabet most commonly used to write the Sanskrit language. The following is the list of Devanagari characters and their Romanized equivalents that have been used to transliterate the *Narad Bhakti Sutra.* Many Sanskrit sounds do not occur in European languages, so examples have been given of sounds that are similar.

Vowels

Each of these Devanagari letters represents only one vowel sound:

अ	**a** as in **a**ffectionate	ऐ	**ai** as in pr**ay**
आ	**ā** as in c**a**lm	ओ	**o** as in b**ow**l
इ	**i** as in f**i**ckle	औ	**au** as in **ow**ner
ई	**ī** as in fr**ee**	ऋ	**ṛ** as in dr**i**nk
उ	**u** as in b**oo**k	ॠ	**ṝ** as in gr**ie**f
ऊ	**ū** as in fr**ui**tful	अं	**aṁ** as in French *bon*
ए	**e** as in unf**e**ttered	अः	**aḥ** as in **a h**ug

Consonants

Each Devanagari character in this set represents a full Sanskrit syllable: a consonant plus "schwa," pronounced like the short "a" in an unstressed syllable in English. Transcription and examples are listed for the consonant sound only.

क	**k** as in lu**ck**	ग	**g** as in **g**ood
ख	**kh** as in **c**afe	घ	**gh** as in do**g h**ouse

ङ	**ṅ** as in you**ng**	न	**n** as in Spanish ***niño***
च	**c** as in **ch**uckle	प	**p** as sto**p**
छ	**ch** as in cat**ch**er	फ	**ph** as **p**uddle
ज	**j** as in **j**umble	ब	**b** as in **b**ountiful
झ	**jh** as in he**dgeh**og	भ	**bh** as in gra**b h**ands
ञ	**ñ** as in ba**ny**an	म	**m** as in **m**ud
ट	**ṭ** as in hear**t**	य	**y** as in **y**ummy
ठ	**ṭh** as in ar**th**ouse	र	**r** as in Spanish *rio*
ड	**ḍ** as in ar**d**or	ल	**l** as in **l**ove
ढ	**ḍh** as in goo**d h**arvest	व	**v** as in **v**ine
ण	**ṇ** as in bar**n**acle	श	**ś** as in **sh**awl
त	**t** as in Spanish ***ta**basco*	ष	**ṣ** as in har**sh**
थ	**th** as **t** with more breath	स	**s** as in **s**ubmarine
द	**d** as in Spanish ***d**ama*	ह	**h** as in **h**umble
ध	**dh** as **d** with more breath		

Bengali and Braj Bhasha

For ease of pronunciation, diacritic markings have been adapted slightly from the preceding list for the Bengali and Braj Bhasha songs. च/চ has been rendered *cha*, while छ/ছ becomes *ćha*; श/শ is written as *śha*, and ष/ষ as *ṣha*. In these songs, the English letter "a" is dropped at the ends of words, to reflect the way these languages are pronounced by native speakers. The nasals *anusvāra* and *candrabindu* are represented by the characters *ň* and *ń*, respectively.

CPSIA information can be obtained at www.ICGtesting.com
Printed in the USA
BVOW02s0458191213

339207BV00002B/22/P

9 780989 143301